Beckett PR...

HOT WHEELS™

BECKETT
B
MEDIA

Beckett Media
4635 McEwen Rd.
Dallas, TX 75244
972-991-6657

www.Beckett.com/HotWheels
Go to www.hotwheels.com/cars to track your Hot Wheels cars online.

CONTENTS

PUBLISHED BY BECKETT MEDIA LLC

EDITORIAL
VP of Development Bridgett Hurley
bhg@beckett.com

Editorial Director Doug Kale
Editor Tim Trout
Editorial Staff Chris Olds, Jason Winter
Art Director Eric Knagg
Art Staff Chelsea Harrison, Tom Carroll
Digital Studio Daniel Moscoso

SPORTS DATA PUBLISHING
Director of Data Publishing Bill Sutherland
Sports Data Publishing Manager Dan Hitt
Sr. Market Analysts Brian Fleischer, Keith Hower, Tim Trout, Bryan Hornbeck
Price Guide Staff Jeff Camay

SALES & MARKETING
Director of Sports Marketing Brad Hastedt
Advertising Sales Misti Floyd, Todd Westover, Brett Robertson, Patty Burrell, Karen Sisler, David Beckler
Advertising Coordination Patty Burrell (Manager)
Dealer Sales Tim Yoder

TECHNOLOGY GROUP
IT Director Joe Rappe

WEB COMMERCE AND SERVICES GROUP
Web Commerce Staff Traci Kaplan, Dave Sliepka, Aaron Gibson
Beckett Grading Services Director Mark Anderson
Beckett Grading Services Staff Jeromy Murray (Operations Manager), Scott Kirklen (Grader Manager), J.J. Arrendondo, Keven Bajraszewski, Eddie Brandon, Andy Broome, Joe Clemons, Steve Dalton, Rosanna Gonzalez, Matt McCliment, Luis Mellado, Paul Moscoso, Aram Munoz, Brian Nelson, David Poole, David Porras, Roberto Ramirez, Brad Grmela

LOGISTICS AND DISTRIBUTION
Albert Chavez (Senior Manager), Uno Kevric, Toli Strakh, Sebastien Rueda, Ana Riano

A BECKETT MEDIA LLC COMPANY
Founder & Advisor Dr. James Beckett III
President Brian Gulledge
Senior Vice President Circulation Nick Singh
Senior Vice President Sales & Marketing Mike Obert

E-mail us: HotWheels@Beckett.com

A BECKETT MEDIA LLC COMPANY

SPECIAL THANKS TO: Mattel's Hot Wheels staff and Rob Graves of southtexasdiecast.com for providing a lot of images and information for this book.

An Exclusive Interview with Hot Wheels R/C Designer York Bleyer

By Doug Kale

York Bleyer

Q: When did you begin working for Mattel and what were some of your first car designs?

A: April 2007, I worked with our designers on a number of RC (remote controlled) products. The Turbo Wheelie Cycle, Fire Bolt RC.

You can now find one of our newest products on the shelves called Stealth Rides. We're really proud of them. They're all new original Hot Wheels designs of R/C Cars and Power Tread vehicles. Totally amazing, they transform from flat to fat, and the best part is you can take them anywhere you go in their remote control storage transmitter case.

Q: Can you describe what your job is like at Mattel and what area of the production process you work on?

A: The Hot Wheels RC team's main focus is to generate new ideas, new toys, and new ways to play, while maintaining the true spirit of a Hot Wheels car.

My job is very fast-paced with plenty to do. It's never boring as there is always a new project to complete.

Really, the creative process starts with a simple idea. Then we create a visual sketch or drawing of what we may think the toy could look like and or work like. From that point we build a working rough model of

how the new toy could function. After we refine how the toy works and we are sure that it puts a smile on a child's face we go with it.

Creating a fun toy takes much more effort then you can imagine. So many people are involved at so many different levels. It's never a one-person job. It takes a very long list of skill sets by people to produce a great toy. It can take any number of designers, mechanical and electrical engineers, sales and marketing people, the list goes on and on. Our jobs are all about team work and supporting a common goal or vision.

Q: Are there many Hot Wheels cars designs that don't make it to production or are they all used at some point in time?

A: It all depends. There are many considerations to keep in mind. In most cases we start out with a basic idea or guideline. We might explore a bit with a number of different design directions, but as we gain a greater understanding of the constraints and strategies, we may modify or change the product offering or line up for that specific season.

Q: In your opinion, what are the top three most popular Hot Wheels cars on the shelves today?

A: The trend changes all the time. If I'm not mistaken, I know the Bone Shaker and '60s era Camaro have always been a hot topic with the public.

Q: Over the years there have been a lot of wacky designs in the Hot Wheels brand. What would you say is the most unusual-looking Hot Wheels car released to date?

A: If wacky is the category, "Hot Tub" hands down! Other then that I'd have to go with any of the creature-based designs, just wild. It is very inspiring once you realize how creative the human mind can be.

Q: Is there one particular Hot Wheels car that is your favorite of all time?

A: This really comes down to personal preference. I have two favorite designs for very different reasons. My first choice is the "Prototype H-24" in British racing green, pure in its references to a classic era in automotive racing/design. My second choice is the "Solar Reflex", a radical spin on the future of where automotive design could go. You

York and Sean

may or may not like the idea of an alternative fuel vehicle in the future. But it's all about exploration of the possibilities, very cool!

Q. Are you a collector of Hot Wheels cars, as well? If so, which car is the most valuable or rarest in your collection?

A: Yes, I have a number of the different designer creations that I plan to pass down to my son when he is old enough. I don't really place a monetary value on the individual car. For me it is as simple as, "Do I like the design enough to collect it?"

Q: Did you play with cars when you were a boy? If so, what types were they?

A: Hot Wheels, what else? Truth be told, though, as I got older I spent a lot of time building plastic models. Kit "bashing" we would call it. I would take a number of parts from several different model kits and build my very own designs.

Q: What type of car do you drive today?

A: My family and I like to explore in the outback when we travel. Our main vehicle is a 2010 Nissan Xterra. We also enjoy our dirt bikes when we travel/ride as a family.

Q: If someone wanted to work in the toy industry as a designer such as yourself, what type of suggestions or recommendations would you give them?

A: I have to think about this question a bit?

If I think about it there are a few a common characteristics that most designers share.

We are driven and like to solve problems. If a task needs to be done we figure out a way to accomplish it when others may be not willing.

We are curious by nature and like to explore. We seek out the opportunity to make things better or improve anything from a design to a process.

We like to have fun. We turn a task into a challenge and make it fun. We work with so many different people around the world and that really fun.

We are creative. We are always looking for new ways to create and express our ideas.

Some days it might mean painting, drawing, sculpting, welding, or working on the computer. It just depends what kind of mood you're in?

Thank you for a great interview!

STEALTH RIDES

Have you seen the the coolest new product from the makers of Hot Wheels? It's called Stealth Rides. Each car folds and fits in a case that doubles as a remote. You've never seen a Remote Control (RC) do that before! Plus they're portable. You can take it anywhere and it fits in your pocket. The Stealth Rides has Racing Cars for speed and racing and Power Treads for climbing and battling.

CHECK IT OUT!

RACING CAR
VERSION 1

Small enough to fit in a pocket, Stealth Rides™ are engineered to amaze! This mini but mighty R/C Racing Car™ folds flat and fits in a slim carrying case – but don't be fooled! The carrying case doubles as the controller! Slide the vehicle from the controller and with one press of a button, transform it to a full-functional R/C vehicle! Built for high speed turns and spinning, Stealth Rides™ Racing Car™ is the biggest little thing in the world of R/C! Collect 'em all!

SRP: $24.99

Ages: 8+

Available: Now

Collecting Hot Wheels cars is a hobby that is enjoyed by people all over the world. These cars have been a favorite toy of kids and adults since 1968 and continue to be very popular today.

Because Hot Wheels cars are found in almost every store selling toys, starting a collection is easy. How, what and where to collect are questions that are asked by many new collectors. Here are some tips and guidelines that may help answer these questions.

KEEPING CARS IN OR OUT OF THE PACKAGE

Cars that are kept in their original packages are always more collectible and their value is usually much higher than with cars that are opened and played with. The most desired cars by collectors usually have perfect packaging (no bent corners or other defects). Many collectors store their packaged cars in clear cases that are specially designed to protect and hold Hot Wheels cars.

Opening Hot Wheels cars decreases their value, but increases their play value. They're much easier to display and can be stored much easier. It is much more fun to be able to play with and race cars on a track set than looking at them through a package. There are many different types of cases available to neatly store loose cars together.

COLLECTING BY SERIES OR COLLECTOR NUMBERS

Since 1995, Hot Wheels cars have been released as part of several different series each year. These include new models, Treasure Hunts, and segment series. These are easy to identify and are clearly labeled on the packaging. The balance of the released cars each year are called regular issue or open stock.

New Models are Hot Wheels designs that have appeared for the very first time. These are also known as first editions.

Segment Series include cars that are grouped by special themes.

Treasure Hunts cars are randomly packed in case assortments and are highly desired by collectors. There are 12 different cars released in this series each year.

Regular issues are cars that aren't part of any series or theme. They usually only have a collector number and car name on the packaging. These cars were issued prior to 2002, where all cars have been inserted into a designated segment series.

Every released car has a collector number which makes it easy to organize them in numerical order.

IDENTIFYING THE SEGMENTS

Here's a helpful guide to identifying the different segments of Hot Wheels cars.

2010 New Models

First time ever in the Hot Wheels line (look for the yellow stripe)

Treasure Hunt

Grab them if you see them, because these Trea$ure Hunt$ are hard to find (look for the green stripe)

Track Stars

Our top track star performers (look for the orange stripe)

Mystery

Life is like a Mystery car...since the blister is black, you never know what you're gonna get. (look for the black stripe)

Race World

Some of the coolest car themes you could race include: Beach, CITY, Movie Stunts and Speedway. (look for the red stripe)

All Stars

Some of the all-time favorites (look for the blue stripe)

10 Groups of 10

2011 Treasure Hunt

2011 Super Treasure Hun

COLLECTING SIMILAR STYLES, DESIGNS OR COLORS

Many people collect only certain styles or models of cars. They may have a favorite color they like or a special car they dream of owning one day. This type of collection is more personal and is usually the most enjoyable.

VARIATIONS

Sometimes a car with the same collector number or series will be released with a different body color, window color, interior color, wheels, or graphic design. The result of these changes can turn out to be a very limited release and are highly sought after by collectors.

WHERE TO FIND HOT WHEELS CARS

Newer releases can all be found at most retail stores that carry toys. These stores usually have a great selection of cars to choose from and also sell related gift sets, track sets, and play sets.

Previously released cars are harder to find at retail stores. Collectors usually look for older cars at garage/yard sales, estate sales, and at local Hot Wheels clubs. Flea Markets, Toy Shows, and online auction sites are also good places to find older releases.

HOT WHEELS CLUBS

There are clubs, dedicated to collecting Hot Wheels cars, throughout the world. These clubs usually have monthly meetings and are very family oriented. Many clubs are usually very helpful to new collectors by promoting the hobby, relaying the latest information on car availability, and organizing Hot Wheels related activities. This may include downhill races, buying/selling/trading and Hot Wheels customizing.

SPOT THE TREAS HUNT DIFFERENC

Here are three ways if you have a regular Treasure Hunt or a Sup Treasure Hunts.

1. Look at the photo ri above. Notice the "S" i word Treasure? If it has "$" dollar sign instead o "S" it's a Super Treasure Hunt.

2. Take a look at the w in both packages. The Treasure Hunt wheels either made of rubber, ture special hubcaps o include more detail tha regular TH version.

3. The paint on a Sup Treasure Hunt is usual duced with a hard-to-fi metallic color.

WHEEL IDENTIFICATION GUIDE

Here's the complete list for all wheel variations. Each wheel is assigned a code (an abbreviation) for use in the following pages in our pictorial price guide.

10SP
10-Spoke Wheel

10SPBLING
Bling 10-Spoke Wheel

3SP
3-Spoke

5DOT
5 Dot (5DOT) or 5 Hole (5HOLE)

5SP
5-Spoke

5SPBLING
Bling 5-Spoke Wheel

6SPBLING
Bling 6-Spoke Wheel

7SP
7-Spoke

BFG5SP
BF Goodrich 5-Spoke

BFGRR
BF Goodrich Real Riders

BlackGY5SP
Black 5-Spoke w/ 'Goodyear'

BlackGY7SP
Black 7-Spoke w/ 'Goodyear'

BLING
Bling 'Spinner Type' Wheel

BW
Basic Wheels or Black Walls

CM6
Co-Molded Wheel 6-Spoke

CoMo
Co-Molded Wheel

Corgi
Corgi Wheel Style 1

Corgi
Corgi Wheel Style 2

CT
Construction Tires

FTE
Faster Than Ever

GHO
Gold Hot Ones

GY5SP
5-Spoke w/ 'Goodyear'

GY7SP
7-Spoke w/ 'Goodyear'

GYBW
Basic Wheels w/ 'Goodyear'

GYRR
Real Riders w/ 'Goodyear'

HH
Hot Hub

HO
Hot Ones

LIW
Lime Wheels

MGW
Micro Gear Wheels

Micro5SP
Micro 5-Spoke Wheel

OH5SP
Open Hole 5-Spoke

OR5SP
Off-Road 5-Spoke

**ORCT** Off-Road Construction Tires	**ORMC** Off-Road Motorcycle	**ORRR** Off-Road Real Riders (Grey or White Hubs)	**ORSB** Off-Road Sawblade or Directional
PC5 5-Spoke Pro Circuit	**PC6** 6-Spoke Pro Circuit	**PCOM** Power Command	**POW** Progressive Oval
PR5 Named after Phil Riehlman	**RLA** Red Line or Red Stripe 1968-1977	**RLB** Red Line or Red Stripe 1973-1977 (retooled in 2007)	**RLC** Red Line 2002-Present
RL5SP Red Line 5-Spoke	**RL7SP** 7-Spoke w/Red Line	**RLRR** Red Line Real Riders	**RR** Real Riders (Grey or White Hubs)
RR5SP 5-Spoke Mag Style Real Riders	**RR6SP** 6-Spoke Real Riders	**RRBNG** BNG Real Rider	**RRMAG** Mag Style Real Riders
RRPrf Prefered Series Real Riders	**SB** Sawblade or Directional	**ScPR5** Screamin' PR5 Wheel	**SCW** Screamin' Wheels
SK5 Skinny Wheel	**SS5SP** Street Show 5-Spoke	**SSO5SP** Street Show Open 5-Spoke	**TW** Turbo Wheels
UH Ultra Hots	**WLRR** White Line Real Riders	**WSP** Wire Spoke (WSP) or Lace Wheels (LW)	**WW** Basic White Wall
WWRR White Wall Real Riders	**Y5** 'Y' 5-Spoke Wheel	**MC3** Motorcycle 3-Spoke	**MC5** Motorcycle 5-Spoke

*Listings in the price guide will have the color added to the wheel description. For example: GoldSP or Blue5Dot.

HOT WHEELS COLLECTOR CLUBS
Attend a club in your area!

Birmingham, AL
Heart of Dixie Hotwheelers
Paul Douglas
mpdouglas@charter.net

Dothan, AL
Deepsouth_Diecast
Phil (hotwheelphil)
psakers1970@graceba.net

Huntsville, AL
Rocket City Hotwheelers
Joe Davis / joed@charter.net

Jasper, AL
Outlaw Hot Wheels
Ted / ted_m_lynn@msn.com

Bentonville, AR
Central States Hot Wheel Club
Randy Wilson
hotwheeler41@yahoo.com

Little Rock, AR
Rock City Redliners
Shawn Neel
rockcityredliners@yahoo.com

Buenos Aires, Argentina
Revolucion Hot Wheels®
Sergio Porchakis
revolucionhotwheels@gmail.com

Buenos Aires, Argentina
Autos a escala
http://autosescala.foroes.net/
Carlos Casciani
charlyc_22@hotmail.com

Buenos Aires, Argentina
Hot Wheels American Club
Gustavo Capozzi
guspat2000@gmail.com

Buenos Aires, Argentina
Diecast Collectors Argentina
Charly Girola / charlygirola@yahoo.com

Cordoba, Argentina
Hot Wheels Argentina
Pablo Jose Posadas
hobby_cba@hotmail.com

Mesa/Gilbert, AZ
Xtreme Lowz AZ Hot Wheelz Club
Jim Powers
xtremelowzhwc@cox.net

Phoenix, AZ
Arizona Outlaws Hot Wheels Collectors Club
Wayne Henderson
azoutlaws@cox.net

Phoenix, AZ
Wheels of Fire Hot Wheels Club
Ken Adams
H.W.Teched@cox.net

Yuma, AZ
Hot Wheels of Yuma
Jeff Hitchens
AZHitch03@aol.com
Romero39@juno.com

Curitiba, Brazil
Hot Wheels Brasil
Anderson Amin
amiansiman@yahoo.com.br

Curitiba, Brazil
Hot Wheels Collectors Brazil
Edson Quadros
edson@hwc.com.br

Pao Paulo, Brazil
CPCVM
Alexandre Bruno - Fire_Fox

Rio De Janeiro, Brazil
Clube Hot Wheels® Brasil
Marcelo DT
Admin
dt@clubehotwheelsbrasil.com.br

Albany, CA
Bay Area Diecas Association
QyvQyv AKA Kife
SorensenProperties@yahoo.com

Bakersfield, CA
MOHWC
Mike Scales
mscales@sbcglobal.net

Eureka, CA
Redwood Coast Diecast Club
Andrew Howard
hemoparkidd@yahoo.com

Laguna Niguel, CA
So-Cal Originals
Mike Hutton
mike@socaloriginals.com

Riverside, CA
Hot Rod Hot Wheelers of the Inland Empire
Richard Whitmark
nwhitmark@surfside.net

Riverside, CA
Jurupa Mountain Hot Wheels
Chelle Smith / HOTWHEELZGRL@aol.com

San Jose, CA
Northern California Hot Wheels Club
Luciano Torres
norcalhotwheels@sbcglobal.net

Colorado Springs, CO
Pikes Peak Hot Wheelers
Paul / pabrada@att.net

Denver, CO
Rocky Mountain Hot Wheelers
Peter Kistler / President
info@rmhwc.org

Loveland, CO
Colorado Diecast Collectors
Lance Comings
coloradodiecast@aol.com

Bogota, Colombia
Coleccionistas de Hot Wheels Colombia
Sachi Alberto
clubhotwheelscolombia@hotmail.com

Middletown, CT
Southern New England Hot Wheelers (SNEHW)
Al / Tatumahn@aol.com

Windsor Locks, CT
CT. Valley Die-cast (C.V.D)
Ken / cwik111@yahoo.com

Crestview, Fl
Hub City Car Club
Kevin Smithsandy054@centurytel.net

Homestead, FL
South Florida Hot Wheels® Collectors Club
Jon Wasielewski
jon@sfloridahotwheelscollectorsclub.com

Jacksonville, FL
First Coast Hot Wheels Collectors
James Hudgins
james@firstcoasthotwheels.com

Lehigh, FL
Hot Wheel Collectors of Southwest
Florida
Ken / 239-369-2708 or 239-292-5756

St. Petersburg, FL
Suncoast Diecasters
Mike Freeland
bigtractormike1@tampabay.rr.com

Tallahassee, FL
Tallahassee Hot Wheels® Club
James Graves / gfieldj@aol.com

Tampa Bay, FL
Tampa Bay Hot Wheels Club
Matthew
727-992-4921/ jerabeks@live.com

Atlanta, GA
Peachstate Hot Wheels
Robby / robbyswheels@yahoo.com

Münster, Germany
Hot Wheels Collectors Germany
HWCG
gn@hotwheelscollectors.de

Budapest, Hungary
Hot Wheels Club - Hungary
Soós Csaba (hotwheels71)
hotwheelshun@gmail.com

Des Moines, IA
All Iowa Hot Wheels Collectors Club
Steve Dippold
steve67GTO@msn.com

Fort Dodge, IA
Fort Dodge Area Hot Wheels
Collectors
Calvin Stewart
stewfam@lvcta.com

Hayden, ID
Northwest Die-cast Collectors Club
Rick Fristoe
nwdiecastclub@aol.com

Chicago, IL
Windy City Hot Wheelers
Jay Milkeris
xxtunemanxx@hotmail.com

Peoria, IL
Central Illinois Hot Wheels Club
Shane Schofield
centralillinoishotwheelsclub@insightbb.com

Evansville, IN
River City Hot Wheelers
Pete Tobin
pktobin@insightbb.com

Indianapolis, IN
Indy Hot Wheels Club
Dave Koch
littlemkk@yahoo.com

Muncie, IN
East Central Indiana
Hot Wheels Club
Brian/April Hanaway
ecihwc@yahoo.com

South Bend, IN
Michiana Hot Wheelers
Jim Baldwin
jabaldwin1@verizon.net

Kansas City, KS
MO-KAN Hotwheelers
Kevin Zwart
kzcars@yahoo.com

Benton, KY
Bluegrass Hot Wheels Club
ptrob@vci.net

Louisville, KY
Derby City Hot Wheelers
bigloucat@bellsouth.net

Braintree, MA
Boston Area Toy Collectors Club
Stephen Lanzilla
781-963-0615

Southboro, MA
East Coast Real Riders
Joe Small
fgxl500@aol.com

Baltimore, MD
Chesapeake Bay Hot Wheels Club
Joel Buckner
cowboy20000@msn.com

Baltimore, MD
The Charm City Collector's Club - C4
c4hotwheels@c4hotwheels.tk

Edgemere, Md
Charm City Collectors Club
James Goolsbee / goolz11@hotmail.com

Bangor, ME
Eastern Maine Diecast Association
Roger Priest / Rpriest@maine.edu

D.F, Mexico
Hot Wheels Nascar
Hotwheelsnascar@yahoogrupos.com.mx

Guadalajara, Mexico
Wheels Collector
Elias / gumaro.elias@gmail.com

Mexico City, Mexico
The All New Die-Cast Cars Collectors
Sergio de la Garza Hernandez
sergiogarzahdez@hotmail.com

Mexico City, Mexico
Hot Wheels® Collectors
Mexico y mas
Constantino Lopez Hdz.
yaxley99@yahoo.com

Mexico City, Mexico
Hot Wheels Collectors Mania
Alfredo Mendez y. Rock
HotwheelsCollectorsMania@hotmail.com

Mexico City, Mexico
Jaapwheels
jaaphotwheels@yahoogrupos.com.mx

Mexico City, Mexico
Hot Wheels Mexico Club
Juan Carlos Lara
jaguar9@hotwheelsmexicoclub.com

Monterrey, Mexico
Capitulo Monterrey de Hot Wheels
Arturo Morales / jarturo76@yahoo.com

Monterrey, Mexico
Union de Coleccionistas
Hot Wheels de Monterrey
Luis Carlos Montemayor
luigicharlesmonteveli@hotmail.com

Detroit, MI
Motor City Hot Wheelers
Sheri Abbey
lca@tir.com

Fraser, MI
Fraytown Redliners
Dave Griff
gobluegriff@yahoo.com

Rochester, MI
Mid-Michigan Hot Wheel Nuts
Bob Duffney / Bobfrmct@yahoo.com

Kansas City, MO
MO-KAN Hotwheelers
Kevin Zwart
kzcars@yahoo.com

St. Louis, MO
Gateway Hot Wheelers Club
Robert Wicker
ghwcrobert@aol.com

Columbus, MT
Big Sky Hot Wheels®
Richard
rwbmcduff@aol.com

Raleigh / Greensboro, NC
East Coast Hot Wheels Club
Rick Putek
rputek@charter.net

Plaistow, NH
Northern New England Hot Wheelers
Phil Davis
phillipdavis@yahoo.com

Ridgewood, NJ
**New Jersey Diecast
Collector's Club (NJDCC)**
Ken Packowski
cgmgd@allstate.com
President

Albuquerque, NM
Roadrunners Collector Club
Curtis Moseley
cnmhotwheels@cs.com

Deer Park, NY
New York Hot Wheelers Club
Frank Abadie
fabayport@aol.com

Boardman, OH
MVHWC
Mike
mike_61443@yahoo.com

Columbus, OH
Central Ohio Hot Wheels Club
Patrick Hardina
teddytiggr@aol.com

Dayton, OH
Exclusively Hot Wheels Club
Roger Chappel
r.chappel@comcast.net

Marysville, OH
**Hot Wheels Collector Club of
Marysville**
Jame Story
Thestory6583@sbcglobal.net

Medina, OH
**NEOHC - North East Ohio Hotwheels
Collectors**
Gary Frederick
neohwc@verizon.net

Shelby, OH
Mid-Ohio Hot Wheelers Club
John Bloom
jbloom@neo.rr.com

Tulsa, OK
Klub Kool Stuff
Kris
Darryl

Tulsa, OK
T-Town Wheelers
Robert Priebe
coolwheels@valornet.com

Salem, OR
Mid-Valley Hotwheelers Club
Larry Webb
webb6@hotmail.com

Allentown, PA
Pennsylvania Hot Wheels Association
djyr2003@gmail.com

Cranberry, PA
Steel City Diecast Club
Rick Sobek
rjlsobek@connecttime.net

Monroeville, PA
Iron City Wheelers
Shane Whittenbarger
info@ironcitywheelers.com

Caguas, PR
Puerto Rico Die Cast Collectors Club
Carmelo Toledo
cobracee@prtc.net

Ensenada, PR
Collectors & Racing Hot Wheels Club
Alex Torres
alexhotwheels@hotmail.com

Cranston, RI
Rhode Island Hot Wheels Club
Jim Lombardi
JLHotwheel@cox.net

Anderson, SC
Palmetto State Hot Wheels® Club
Jim Pietrowski/redryder31
redryder31@charter.net

Darlington, SC
East Coast Hot Wheels Club
Jason Patterson
crewchief4344@juno.com

Saskatoon, SK, CAN
Prairiefire Hot Wheels Club
John Turanich
prairiefirehwc@hotmail.com

Knoxville, TN
East Tennessee Hot Wheelers
Tim Brantley
timsseadoo@aol.com

Memphis, TN
Hot Wheels Collectors of Memphis
Greg
hwcmemphis@hotmail.com

Austin, TX
Bat City Hot Wheels Collectors
Bob Ratliff
batcityhwc@austin.rr.com

Dallas/Ft Worth, TX
North Texas Diecast Collectors Club
Tommy
northtexasdiecast@yahoo.com

Houston, TX
**Space City Hot Wheels®
Collectors Club**
Chuck Gronemeyer
chuck@spacecityhw.com

San Angelo, TX
San Angelo Diecast Collectors Club
Leonard Manis
ljm72@yahoo.com

San Antonio, TX
South Texas Diecast Collectors
www.southtexasdiecast.com

Salt Lake City, UT
Salt Flat Hot Wheelers
Randy Muir / flyingmur@msn.com

Roanoke, VA
Star City Hot Wheels®
Tim Whitlock
starcityhotwheels@cox.net

Roanoke/Lynchburg, VA
East Coast Hot Wheels Club
Carl Crawford / crayfish3609@aol.com

Winchester, VA
**Winchester/Shenandoah Valley Hot
Wheels Club**
Dan Hammond / hwdan2@earthlink.net

Republic, WA
**Hot Wheels Collectors Club of
Washington**
Richard Guilliot
hotwheelsclub@hotmail.com

Milwaukee, WI
Milwaukee Hot Wheels Club
Rob Johnston
GTR-Rob@sbcglobal.net

Oshkosh, Wi
Fox Cities Diecast
Fred Dunlop
foxcitiesdiecast@hotmail.com

Bridgeport, WV
Mountaineer Hot Wheels® Club
Scott Reppert - mountaineer
hwc@hotmail.com

BECKETT HOT WHEELS PRICE GUIDE

HOW TO GRADE YOUR HOT WHEELS CARS COLLECTION

ONLY A GUIDE Beckett listings are to be used only as a guide. The prices do not represent an offer to buy or sell on the part of any party.

HOW PRODUCTS ARE LISTED All Hot Wheels cars listed in this guide are 1:64 scale. WalMart, Target, Kmart and Toys R Us have each had their share of exclusive Hot Wheels cars. We've noted those in the Price Guide listings.

Here's a sample of the guide:

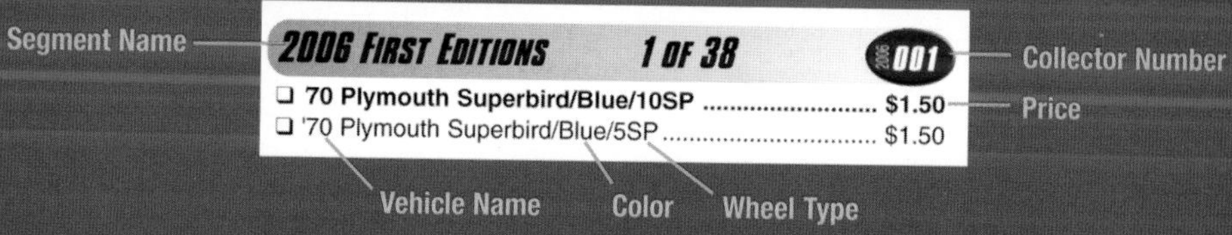

Segment Name

2006 FIRST EDITIONS	1 OF 38	001

Collector Number

❏ **70 Plymouth Superbird/Blue/10SP** $1.50
❏ '70 Plymouth Superbird/Blue/5SP $1.50

Price

Vehicle Name — Color — Wheel Type

CONDITION GUIDE

Most Hot Wheels products are sold in their original packaging. Due to variations and descriptions, packaging is sometimes as important as the die-cast vehicle itself. Prices listed are for unblemished die-cast products in their original, undamaged packaging.

Here are some guidelines to determine conditions:

Mint (MT)
A vehicle and package that has no blemishes is considered Mint. The item looks like it just rolled off the manufacturing line. Mint Hot Wheels cars are valued at 125% of this guide.

Near Mint – Mint (NmMT)
This vehicle has a very tiny flaw along the edge of the packaging or a price sticker residue. NmMT Hot Wheels cars are valued at 100% of this guide.

Near Mint (NRMT)
This is a vehicle with one very minor flaw. Any one of the following would lower a Mint piece to NRMT: decals on the vehicle being slightly smudged, barely noticeable scratches on the packaging, a small bend in the packaging. NRMT Hot Wheels cars are valued at 75-90% of this guide.

Excellent (EX)
This is a vehicle with noticeable defects or wear. Any of the following would be characteristics of an EX die-cast piece: wrinkled decals, paint smudges, packaging with easily noticeable scratches or wear. EX die-casts are valued at 50-75% of this guide.

Good (G)
This is a vehicle with major defects or wear. All of the following would lower a vehicle to G: Faded decals, a loose wheel, scratches on the die-cast, packaging with several creases. G die-casts are valued at 25-50% of this guide.

Poor (P)
This is a vehicle that has been well-used or abused. A vehicle in this condition usually has been taken out of the packaging and been played with. Characteristics of P are: scratched off decals, dents in the die-cast, scratches all over the die-cast, unattractive and mutilated boxes. P die-casts are valued at 5-25% of this guide.

Vehicles Without Packaging (Loose)
Die-casts without original packaging and in Mint condition are valued at 40-50% of this guide.

Segment Vehicle Number

Hot Wheels Logo

J3252
011

Nerve Hammer 11/38

Vehicle Name

Blister

Product Year, Collector Number

2006 FIRST EDITIONS
1.1 OF 38

3+

2006 FIRST EDITIONS   **1 OF 38**   2006 **001**

❏ '70 Plymouth Superbird/Blue/10SP $1.50
❏ '70 Plymouth Superbird/Blue/5SP $1.50

2006 FIRST EDITIONS   **1 OF 38**   2006 **001**

❏ '70 Plymouth Superbird/Copper/10SP $30.00
❏ **'70 Plymouth Superbird/Copper/PR5 ......** $1.50

2006 FIRST EDITIONS — 1 OF 38 — 2006 001

- ❑ '70 Plymouth Superbird/Green/10SP $1.50
- ❑ **'70 Plymouth Superbird/Green/5SP $1.50**
- ❑ '70 Plymouth Superbird/Green/FTE $4.00

2006 FIRST EDITIONS — 1 OF 38 — 2006 001

- ❑ **'70 Plymouth Superbird/Yellow/10SP...... $1.50**
- ❑ '70 Plymouth Superbird/Yellow/5SP $25.00
- ❑ '70 Plymouth Superbird/Yellow/FTE $25.00

2006 FIRST EDITIONS — 2 OF 38 — 2006 002

- ❑ Toyota AE-86 Corolla/Flat Grey/FTE $40.00
- ❑ Toyota AE-86 Corolla/Flat Grey/Red5SP $30.00
- ❑ Toyota AE-86 Corolla/White/FTE $4.00
- ❑ Toyota AE-86 Corolla/White/Red3SP $40.00
- ❑ **Toyota AE-86 Corolla/White/Red5SP $1.50**

2006 FIRST EDITIONS — 3 OF 38 — 2006 003

- ❑ **Nissan Silvia S15/M Dark Red/10SP $1.50**
- ❑ Nissan Silvia S15/M Dark Red/FTE $3.00

2006 FIRST EDITIONS — 4 OF 38 — 2006 004

- ❑ Chrysler 300C Hemi/Black/Bling $1.50

2006 FIRST EDITIONS — 4 OF 38 — 2006 004

- ❑ **Chrysler 300C Hemi/M Silver/Bling $1.50**
- ❑ Chrysler 300C Hemi/M Silver/FTE $3.00

2006 FIRST EDITIONS — 5 OF 38 — 2006 005

- ❑ Ferrari 512 M/Blue/FTE lg. 6 .... $4.00
- ❑ Ferrari 512 M/Blue/FTE sm. 6 .... $8.00
- ❑ Ferrari 512 M/Blue/Gold5SP lg. 6 .... $1.50
- ❑ **Ferrari 512 M/Blue/Gold5SP sm. 6 .... $3.00**

2006 FIRST EDITIONS — 5 OF 38 — 2006 005

- ❑ Ferrari 512 M/Grey/Gold5SP lg. 6 .... $1.50
- ❑ **Ferrari 512 M/Grey/Gold5SP sm. 6 .... $1.50**

2006 First Editions — 5 of 38 — 005

- Ferrari 512 M/Red/Gold5SP lg. 6 .... $3.00
- **Ferrari 512 M/Red/Gold5SP sm. 6** $1.50

2006 First Editions — 6 of 38 — 006

- Bone Shaker/Black/5SP $3.00
- Bone Shaker/Black/FTE $15.00
- Bone Shaker/Black/RL5SP $80.00

2006 First Editions — 6 of 38 — 006

- Bone Shaker/Dark Red/5SP $3.00

2006 First Editions — 6 of 38 — 006

- **Bone Shaker/Flat Brown/Gold5SP** $3.00
- Bone Shaker/Flat Brown/Gold5SP
  no country base $4.00
- Bone Shaker/Flat Brown/GoldPR5 .... $4.00

2006 First Editions — 7 of 38 — 007

- '69 Corvette/Dark Red/PR5 .... $1.50

2006 First Editions — 7 of 38 — 007

- **'69 Corvette/M Gold/PR5** $1.50
- '69 Corvette/Pearl White/OH5SP (Kmart) .. $3.00
- '69 Corvette/Pearl White/PR5 (Kmart)...... $40.00

2006 First Editions — 7 of 38 — 007

- '69 Corvette/Yellow/FTE $3.00
- **'69 Corvette/Yellow/PR5** $1.50

2006 First Editions — 8 of 38 — 008

- Porsche Carrera GT/Silver/FTE $3.00
- **Porsche Carrera GT/Silver/OH5SP** $1.50

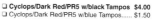

2006 FIRST EDITIONS — 8 OF 38

❏ Porsche Carrera GT/Yellow/OH5SP $1.50
❏ Porsche Carrera GT/Yellow/OH5SP
 w/o back window.................................. $10.00

2006 FIRST EDITIONS — 9 OF 38 009

❏ Cyclops/Dark Red/PR5 w/black Tampos $4.00
❏ Cyclops/Dark Red/PR5 w/blue Tampos...... $1.50

2006 FIRST EDITIONS — 10 OF 38 010

❏ Pharodox/Clear Blue/FTE $3.00
❏ **Pharodox/Clear Blue/GoldOH5SP** $1.50

2006 FIRST EDITIONS — 11 OF 38 011

❏ Nerve Hammer/Clear Red/FTE $3.00
❏ Nerve Hammer/Clear Red/OH5SP $1.50
❏ **Nerve Hammer/Clear Red/OH5SP**
 clear windows $1.50

2006 FIRST EDITIONS — 12 OF 38 012

❏ 2006 Dodge Viper Coupe/M Black/OH5SP $1.50

2006 FIRST EDITIONS — 12 OF 38 012

❏ 2006 Dodge Viper Coupe/M Blue/FTE $4.00
❏ **2006 Dodge Viper Coupe/M Blue/OH5SP** $1.50

2006 FIRST EDITIONS — 12 OF 38 012

❏ 2006 Dodge Viper Coupe/M Orange/OH5SP $1.50

2006 FIRST EDITIONS — 13 OF 38 013

❏ Semi-Psycho/M Orange/OH5SP $1.50

2006 FIRST EDITIONS   *14 of 38*   **014**

❏ Chrysler Firepower Concept/M Dark Blue/10SP $1.50

2006 FIRST EDITIONS   *14 of 38*   **014**

❏ **Chrysler Firepower Concept/M Lt.Blue/10SP $1.50**
❏ Chrysler Firepower Concept/M Lt.Blue/FTE $4.00

2006 FIRST EDITIONS   *15 of 38*   **015**

❏ Unobtainium 1/Flat Black/BLING $1.50
❏ **Unobtainium 1/Flat Black/BLING**
   clear windows **$3.00**

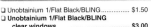

2006 FIRST EDITIONS   *15 of 38*   **015**

❏ Unobtainium 1/Pearl Pink/BLING $1.50

2006 FIRST EDITIONS   *16 of 38*   **016**

❏ AMG-Mercedes-Benz CLK DTM/Black/10SP $1.50

2006 FIRST EDITIONS   *16 of 38*   **016**

❏ **AMG-Mercedes-Benz CLK DTM/M**
   Silver/10SP... **$1.50**
❏ AMG-Mercedes-Benz CLK DTM/M
   Silver/10SP w/o Tampos $1.50
❏ AMG-Mercedes-Benz CLK DTM/M
   Silver/FTE $4.00

2006 FIRST EDITIONS   *17 of 38*   **017**

❏ Qombee/M Blue & White/PR5 .... $1.50

2006 FIRST EDITIONS   *17 of 38*   **017**

❏ Qombee/M Dark Red/PR5 .... $1.50

2006 First Editions — 18 of 38 — 018
- ❑ Preying Menace/Green/FTE $4.00
- ❑ Preying Menace/Green/OH5SP $10.00
- **❑ Preying Menace/Green/PR5 .... $1.50**

2006 First Editions — 19 of 38 — 019
- ❑ Nissan Z/Blue/OrangeCM6 .... $1.50

2006 First Editions — 19 of 38 — 019
- ❑ Nissan Z/Flat Black/RedCM6 .... $1.50

2006 First Editions — 19 of 38 — 019
- ❑ Nissan Z/M Yellow/ChromeCM6 .... $30.00
- **❑ Nissan Z/M Yellow/CM6 .... $1.50**
- ❑ Nissan Z/M Yellow/FTE $4.00

2006 First Editions — 20 of 38 — 020
- ❑ Hammer Sled/M Gold/GoldMC5 .... $1.50

2006 First Editions — 20 of 38 — 020
- **❑ Hammer Sled/M Purple/MC3................... $5.00**
- ❑ Hammer Sled/M Purple/MC5..................... $1.50

2006 First Editions — 20 of 38 — 020
- ❑ Hammer Sled/Red/MC5 .... $1.50

2006 First Editions — 21 of 38 — 021
- **❑ '69 Camaro/M Black/5SP $1.50**
- ❑ '69 Camaro/M Black/FTE........................... $4.00
- ❑ '69 Camaro/M Black/PR5 .... $3.00

- ❑ '69 Camaro/M Orange/PR5 black base .. $3.00
- ❑ '69 Camaro/M Orange/PR5 chrome base .. $1.50

- ❑ '69 Camaro/M Purple/5SP $1.50
- ❑ '69 Camaro/M Red/PR5 .... $4.00

- ❑ Motoblade/Clear Orange/OrangeOH5SP .. $1.50

- ❑ Hummer/Dark Blue/OR5SP red on window $6.00
- ❑ Hummer/Dark Blue/OR5SP white on window $1.50

- ❑ Hummer/Dark Red/OR5SP $1.50

- ❑ Bon Voyage/Lt. Brown/FTE $4.00
- ❑ **Bon Voyage/Lt. Brown/OH5SP** $1.50
- ❑ Bon Voyage/Lt. Brown/OH5SP red wood .. $1.50

- ❑ Corvette C6R/Silver/10SP $12.00
- ❑ **Corvette C6R/Silver/OH5SP** $1.50
- ❑ Corvette C6R/Silver/Y5 .... $6.00

- ❑ Corvette C6R/Yellow/FTE $4.00
- ❑ **Corvette C6R/Yellow/OH5SP** $1.50

2006 FIRST EDITIONS 26 OF 38 026

❏ Hot Tub/Brown/5SP $1.50
❏ Hot Tub/Brown/FTE $4.00

2006 FIRST EDITIONS 27 OF 38 027

❏ Quad Rod/Dark Red/OH5SP $1.50

2006 FIRST EDITIONS 28 OF 38 028

❏ Honda Civic Si/Dark Red/OH5SP $1.50

2006 FIRST EDITIONS 28 OF 38 028

❏ Honda Civic Si/M Gold/GoldO5SP
   Civic on front $6.00
❏ **Honda Civic Si/M Gold/GoldO5SP**
   Civic on rear $1.50

2006 FIRST EDITIONS 28 OF 38 028

❏ Honda Civic Si/M Green/FTE $4.00
❏ Honda Civic Si/M Green/O5SP
   (Sema Edition) $25.00
❏ **Honda Civic Si/M Green/OH5SP** $1.50

2006 FIRST EDITIONS 29 OF 38 029

❏ '70 Dodge Challenger Hemi/Green/PR5 (Kmart) $3.00
❏ '70 Dodge Challenger Hemi/Orange/PR5 .. $3.00
❏ **'70 Dodge Challenger Hemi/Orange/Y5** .. $1.50

2006 FIRST EDITIONS 29 OF 38 029

❏ '70 Dodge Challenger Hemi/Purple/FTE $4.00
❏ **'70 Dodge Challenger Hemi/Purple/PR5** $1.50

2006 FIRST EDITIONS 30 OF 38 030

❏ Med-Evil/Lt. Blue & Orange/FTE $4.00
❏ Med-Evil/Lt. Blue & Orange/OH5SP $1.50
❏ Med-Evil/Lt. Blue/FTE $12.00
❏ **Med-Evil/Lt. Blue/OrangeOH5SP** $1.50

2006 FIRST EDITIONS — 31 OF 38 — 031

- ❑ Nissan Titan/Black/5DOT $3.00
- ❑ Nissan Titan/Black/OH5SP $6.00
- **❑ Nissan Titan/Black/Y5 .... $1.50**

2006 FIRST EDITIONS — 31 OF 38 — 031

- **❑ Nissan Titan/Dark Red/OH5SP $1.50**
- ❑ Nissan Titan/Dark Red/OH5SP KMC $10.00
- ❑ Nissan Titan/Dark Red/Y5 .... $3.00

2006 FIRST EDITIONS — 31 OF 38 — 031

- ❑ Nissan Titan/Grey/FTE $20.00
- **❑ Nissan Titan/Grey/OH5SP $1.50**
- ❑ Nissan Titan/Grey/PR5 .... $25.00

2006 FIRST EDITIONS — 32 OF 38 — 032

- ❑ Dieselboy/Black/OH5SP $1.50
- ❑ Dieselboy/Black/OH5SP black DIESELBOY $3.00
- **❑ Dieselboy/Black/RedOH5SP $6.00**

2006 FIRST EDITIONS — 33 OF 38 — 033

- ❑ Ferrari F430 Spider/Black/PR5 black Interior $20.00
- **❑ Ferrari F430 Spider/Black/PR5 tan interior $1.50**

2006 FIRST EDITIONS — 33 OF 38 — 033

- ❑ Ferrari F430 Spider/Red/FTE $4.00
- **❑ Ferrari F430 Spider/Red/PR5 .... $1.50**

2006 FIRST EDITIONS — 33 OF 38 — 033

- ❑ Ferrari F430 Spider/Yellow/PR5 .... $1.50

2006 FIRST EDITIONS — 34 OF 38 — 034

- ❑ '07 Cadillac Escalade/Black/FTE................ $4.00
- **❑ '07 Cadillac Escalade/Black/OH5SP........ $1.50**
- ❑ '07 Cadillac Escalade/Black/Y5 .... $1.50

2006 FIRST EDITIONS — 34 OF 38 — 034

- ❑ '07 Cadillac Escalade/Pearl White/5DOT .. $1.50
- ❑ **'07 Cadillac Escalade/Pearl White/Y5...... $1.50**

2006 FIRST EDITIONS — 35 OF 38 — 035

- ❑ Mega Thrust/M Orange/FTE $4.00
- ❑ **Mega Thrust/M Orange/OH5SP............... $1.50**

2006 FIRST EDITIONS — 36 OF 38 — 036

- ❑ Datsun 240Z/M Grey/10SP (Kmart) $3.00
- ❑ Datsun 240Z/Pearl White/10SP............... $40.00
- ❑ Datsun 240Z/Pearl White/FTE................. $25.00
- ❑ **Datsun 240Z/Pearl White/Y5 .... $1.50**

2006 FIRST EDITIONS — 36 OF 38 — 036

- ❑ Datsun 240Z/Yellow/10SP $1.50
- ❑ **Datsun 240Z/Yellow/Y5 .... $1.50**

2006 FIRST EDITIONS — 37 OF 38 — 037

- ❑ '55 Chevy Panel/M Dark Blue/PR5 .... $30.00
- ❑ '55 Chevy Panel/M Dark Blue/PR5 black grill $40.00

2006 FIRST EDITIONS — 38 OF 38 — 038

- ❑ Volkswagen Karmann Ghia/M Grey/PR5 $15.00

TREASURE HUNT — 1 OF 12 — 039

- ❑ Asphalt Assault/Red/Bling6SP black base $30.00
- ❑ Asphalt Assault/Red/Bling6SP chrome base $15.00

✔

TREASURE HUNT — 2 OF 12 — 040

- ❑ '40 Ford Coupe/Black & Yellow/RR5SP .. $20.00

TREASURE HUNT 3 OF 12

❑ Sooo Fast/Spectraflame Copper/RLRR5SP $25.00

TREASURE HUNT 4 OF 12

❑ Custom '59 Cadillac/Blue/WWRRBNG
black interior $200.00
❑ **Custom '59 Cadillac/Blue/WWRRBNG
white interior $25.00**

TREASURE HUNT 5 OF 12

❑ Volkswagen New Beetle Cup/Pearl White &
Blue/OrangeRR5SP $25.00

TREASURE HUNT 6 OF 12

❑ '67 Mustang/Pearl White/RR5SP $25.00

TREASURE HUNT 7 OF 12

❑ 1969 Dodge Charger/Orange/RR $40.00

TREASURE HUNT 8 OF 12

❑ Hummer H3T/Gold & Silver/ORRR $10.00

TREASURE HUNT 9 OF 12

❑ CUL8R/Spectraflame Green/CM6 .... $15.00

TREASURE HUNT 10 OF 12

❑ C6 Corvette/Black/GoldRR5SP $20.00

TREASURE HUNT   11 OF 12

❑ Pit Cruiser/M Purple/MC3 .... $15.00
❑ Pit Cruiser/M Purple/MC5 .... $100.00

TREASURE HUNT   12 OF 12

❑ Dairy Delivery/M Olive Green/GoldWLRR $30.00

DRIFT KINGS   1 OF 5

❑ Super Tsunami/Dark Red/GoldPR5............. $1.50

DRIFT KINGS   2 OF 5

❑ 'Tooned Toyota Supra/M Yellow/PR5
   black hood $1.50
❑ 'Tooned Toyota Supra/M Yellow/PR5
   black roof $1.50

DRIFT KINGS   3 OF 5

❑ 24/Seven/Green/PR5................................. $1.50

DRIFT KINGS   3 OF 5

❑ 24/Seven/Red/PR5 .... $1.50

DRIFT KINGS   4 OF 5

❑ Mid Drift/M Blue/10SP $40.00
❑ Mid Drift/M Blue/White10SP $40.00
❑ Mid Drift/M Blue/WhiteY5 .... $1.50

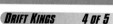

DRIFT KINGS   5 OF 5

❑ Slider/Pearl White/OrangePR5 .... $1.50

DROPSTARS 1 OF 5

❑ Chrysler 300C/M Blue & Champagne/**BLING** $1.50
❑ Chrysler 300C/M Blue & Champagne/FTE
  (Toys R Us Starter) $12.00

DROPSTARS 2 OF 5

❑ Cadillac Cien/Dark M Red/FTE $4.00
❑ Cadillac Cien/Dark M Red/OH5SP $12.00
❑ **Cadillac Cien/Dark M Red/PR5** **$1.50**

DROPSTARS 3 OF 5

❑ Mercedes-Benz G500/M Orange & Black/BLING $1.50

DROPSTARS 4 OF 5

❑ 1964 Impala/Grey & Black/WSP $1.50

DROPSTARS 4 OF 5

❑ 1964 Impala/M Orange & Black/10SP........ $1.50

DROPSTARS 5 OF 5

❑ Nissan Skyline/M Dark Blue/10SP $25.00
❑ **Nissan Skyline/M Dark Blue/OH5SP** **$1.50**

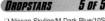

DROPSTARS 5 OF 5

❑ Nissan Skyline/M Grey/OH5SP $1.50

DROPSTARS 5 OF 5

❑ Nissan Skyline/M Teal/O5SP $1.50

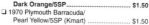

MOPAR MADNESS   1 OF 5   2006 061

❏ 1970 Plymouth Barracuda/M Blue/5SP $1.50

MOPAR MADNESS   1 OF 5   2006 061

❏ **1970 Plymouth Barracuda/M Dark Orange/5SP** **$1.50**
❏ 1970 Plymouth Barracuda/ Pearl Yellow/5SP (Kmart) $1.50
❏ 1970 Plymouth Barracuda/ Pearl Yellow/7SP (Kmart) $80.00

MOPAR MADNESS   2 OF 5   2006 062

❏ Dodge Viper GTS-R/Dark Red/PR5 .... $1.50

MOPAR MADNESS   2 OF 5   2006 062

❏ Dodge Viper GTS-R/M Black/PR5 .... $1.50

MOPAR MADNESS   2 OF 5   2006 062

❏ **Dodge Viper GTS-R/M Yellow/PR5 red interior** **$10.00**
❏ Dodge Viper GTS-R/M Yellow/PR5 yellow interior $1.50

MOPAR MADNESS   3 OF 5   2006 063

❏ Dodge Tomahawk/Red/TMHK $1.50

MOPAR MADNESS   3 OF 5   2006 063

❏ Dodge Tomahawk/White/TMHK $1.50

MOPAR MADNESS   4 OF 5   2006 064

❏ Dodge M80/M Silver/FTE $4.00
❏ **Dodge M80/M Silver/Y5** **$1.50**

MOPAR MADNESS 5 OF 5
❏ 1969 Dodge Charger Daytona/Dark Blue/5SP $1.50

MOPAR MADNESS 5 OF 5
❏ 1969 Dodge Charger Daytona/Lt. Blue/5SP $1.50

CHROME BURNERZ 1 OF 5
❏ Honda Spocket/Chrome/FTE $4.00
❏ **Honda Spocket/Chrome/PR5 .... $1.50**

CHROME BURNERZ 2 OF 5
❏ Humvee/Chrome/OR5SP black & white flames $1.50

CHROME BURNERZ 2 OF 5
❏ Humvee/Chrome/OR5SP green & yellow flames $1.50

CHROME BURNERZ 3 OF 5
❏ **Cockney Cab II/Chrome/OH5SP
  larger rear wheel $1.50**
❏ Cockney Cab II/Chrome/OH5SP
  larger rear wheel
  black windows........................... $1.50
❏ Cockney Cab II/Chrome/OH5SP
  smaller rear wheel................................ $3.00

CHROME BURNERZ 4 OF 5
❏ What-4-2/Chrome/PR5 blue flames............ $1.50

CHROME BURNERZ 4 OF 5
❏ What-4-2/Chrome/PR5 red flames
  chrome engine $1.50
❏ **What-4-2/Chrome/PR5 red flames
  silver engine $1.50**

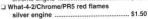

CHROME BURNERZ 5 OF 5
2006 070
❏ Phastasm/Chrome/5SP black interior $12.00
❏ **Phastasm/Chrome/5SP grey interior $1.50**

TAG RIDES 1 OF 5
2006 071
❏ Dairy Delivery/Red/5SP $1.50

TAG RIDES 2 OF 5
2006 072
❏ 1964 Lincoln Continental/Green/WSP $1.50

TAG RIDES 3 OF 5
2006 073
❏ Quadra-Sound/Purple/BLING $1.50

TAG RIDES 4 OF 5
2006 074
❏ Cadillac Sixteen/Yellow/PR5 .... $1.50

TAG RIDES 5 OF 5
2006 075
❏ Hiway Hauler/M Silver/PR5 .... $3.00

SPY FORCE 1 OF 5
2006 076
❏ Boom Box/Black/PR5 .... $1.50

SPY FORCE 2 OF 5
2006 077
❏ Jaguar XK8/M Dark Green/PR5 .... $1.50

SPY FORCE — 3 OF 5 — 2006 — 078

❑ 2001 B Engineering Edonis/Dark Blue/WhitePR5 $1.50

SPY FORCE — 4 OF 5 — 2006 — 079

❑ Combat Ambulance/M Blue-Grey/5SP $1.50
❑ Combat Ambulance/M Blue-Grey/White5SP $1.50

SPY FORCE — 5 OF 5 — 2006 — 080

❑ Lotus Espirit/M Dark Red/FTE.................... $4.00
❑ **Lotus Espirit/M Dark Red/GoldPR5 .... $1.50**

BONE BLAZERS — 1 OF 5 — 2006 — 081

❑ '32 Ford/Flat Black/5SP $1.50

BONE BLAZERS — 2 OF 5 — 2006 — 082
❑ Audacious/Black/FTE $4.00
❑ **Audacious/Black/GoldY5 .... $1.50**

BONE BLAZERS — 3 OF 5 — 2006 — 083

❑ '57 Chevy Bel Air/M Grey/Red3SP $50.00
❑ **'57 Chevy Bel Air/M Grey/Red5SP $1.50**
❑ '57 Chevy Bel Air/M Grey/Red5SP HO $1.50

BONE BLAZERS — 4 OF 5 — 2006 — 084
❑ Rapid Transit/M Red/PR5 .... $1.50

BONE BLAZERS — 5 OF 5 — 2006 — 085

❑ '65 Corvette/Black/5SP $1.50
❑ '65 Corvette/Black/RL5SP $50.00
❑ **'65 Corvette/Black/Y5 .... $1.50**

Hot Wheels

Bone Blazers 5 of 5 — 2006 085
- ❏ '65 Corvette/M Purple/Gold5SP $1.50

Motown Metal 1 of 5 — 2006 086
- ❏ 1970 Chevelle SS/Black/5SP $6.00
- ❏ 1970 Chevelle SS/Black/PR5 black interior $80.00
- **❏ 1970 Chevelle SS/Black/PR5 red interior $5.00**

Motown Metal 1 of 5 — 2006 086
- ❏ 1970 Chevelle SS/Grey/PR5 (Kmart) $4.00
- **❏ 1970 Chevelle SS/Red/PR5 .... $3.00**

Motown Metal 2 of 5 — 2006 087
- ❏ '65 Mustang/Blue/5SP $5.00
- **❏ '65 Mustang/Blue/PR5 .... $5.00**
- ❏ '65 Mustang/Blue/PR5 tinted windows $10.00

Motown Metal 2 of 5 — 2006 087
- ❏ '65 Mustang/Pearl White/Gold10SP $3.00
- ❏ '65 Mustang/Red/PR5 (Kmart) $5.00

Motown Metal 3 of 5 — 2006 088
- ❏ '70 Plymouth Road Runner/
  Lime Green/10SP $3.00
- ❏ '70 Plymouth Road Runner/
  Lime Green/5SP $30.00
- ❏ '70 Plymouth Road Runner/
  M Dark Orange/10SP (Kmart) $30.00
- ❏ '70 Plymouth Road Runner/
  M Dark Orange/5SP (Kmart) $5.00

Motown Metal 4 of 5 — 2006 089
- ❏ 1967 Camaro/Black/5SP $5.00
- ❏ 1967 Camaro/Black/RL5SP..................... $50.00
- **❏ 1967 Camaro/Black/Y5 .... $3.00**

Motown Metal 5 of 5 — 2006 090
- ❏ 1969 Pontiac GTO/Yellow/5SP $1.50

HIGHWAY HORROR 1 OF 5 2006 091

❏ Low Flow/Dark Green & Lt. Green/Gold5SP $1.50

HIGHWAY HORROR 2 OF 5 2006 092

❏ '32 Ford Vicky/Black/PR5, rear BluePR5 .. $1.50

HIGHWAY HORROR 3 OF 5 2006 093

❏ '49 Merc/M Copper/Gold 5SP $1.50

HIGHWAY HORROR 4 OF 5 2006 094

❏ W-Oozie/M Dark Blue/RedMC3.................. $1.50

HIGHWAY HORROR 5 OF 5 2006 095

❏ Rigor Motor/M Magenta/Gold5SP $1.50

RED LINE 1 OF 5 2006 096

❏ Custom '69 Chevy/M Gold/RL5SP (Kmart) $5.00
❏ **Custom '69 Chevy/M Green/RL5SP $3.00**

RED LINE 2 OF 5 2006 097

❏ Ford GT40/M Yellow/RL5SP $1.50

RED LINE 3 OF 5 2006 098

❏ 1968 Nova/M Green/RL5SP (Kmart).......... $5.00
❏ **1968 Nova/M Purple/RL5SP $3.00**

2006

RED LINE   4 OF 5

2006 **099**

❏ Baja Bug/M Red/RL5SP $1.50

RED LINE   5 OF 5

2006 **100**

❏ **1969 Pontiac Firebird T/A/M Blue/RL5SP $3.00**
❏ 1969 Pontiac Firebird T/A/M Magenta/RL5SP $3.00

HI-RAKERS   1 OF 5

2006 **101**

❏ Montezooma/Blue/BLING $1.50

HI-RAKERS   1 OF 5

2006 **101**

❏ Montezooma/Green/BLING black base...... $1.50
❏ **Montezooma/Green/BLING chrome base $3.00**

HI-RAKERS   2 OF 5

2006 **102**

❏ 1971 Buick Riviera/M Purple/PR5 .... $1.50

HI-RAKERS   3 OF 5

2006 **103**

❏ Monte Carlo/M Silver/GoldPR5 .... $1.50

HI-RAKERS   4 OF 5

2006 **104**

❏ '63 Chevy Impala/Green/BLING $1.50

HI-RAKERS   5 OF 5

2006 **105**

❏ Olds 442/M Black/Gold5SP $1.50

WWE — 1 of 5
 2006 **106**

❏ Baja Breaker/Grey Triple H/BlackOR5SP .. $3.00

WWE — 2 of 5
 2006 **107**

❏ '65 Impala/M Green Eddie Guerrero/WSP $3.00

WWE — 3 of 5
 2006 **108**

❏ Ballistik/Flat Black/BlueY5 .... $12.00
❏ **Ballistik/Flat Black/BlueY5 Wrestlemania $3.00**

WWE — 4 of 5
 2006 **109**

❏ Power Panel/M Dark Red Batista/
   Gold5SP $5.00
❏ **Power Panel/M Dark Red Batista/
   GoldOR5SP $3.00**

WWE — 5 of 5
 2006 **110**

❏ Sir Ominous/M Dark Blue Hulk Hogan/RedPR5 $3.00

TRACK ACES — 1 of 12
 2006 **111**

❏ Ferrari 360 Modena/Clear/PR5 .... $1.50

TRACK ACES — 2 of 12
  2006 **112**

❏ Low Carbs/Yellow/5SP $1.50

TRACK ACES — 3 of 12
  2006 **113**

❏ Krazy 8s/Purple/PR5 .... $1.50

TRACK ACES 4 OF 12 114

❑ Stockar/Clear/5SP $1.50

TRACK ACES 5 OF 12 115

❑ Horseplay/Clear Yellow/PR5 .... $1.50

TRACK ACES 6 OF 12 116

❑ Bedlam/Clear Green/FTE $4.00
❑ **Bedlam/Clear Green/PR5** **$1.50**

TRACK ACES 7 OF 12 117

❑ Chevy 1500/Red/5SP $1.50

TRACK ACES 8 OF 12 118

❑ '57 Chevy/Pearl White/5SP $5.00
❑ **'57 Chevy/Pearl White/10SP** **$3.00**

TRACK ACES 9 OF 12 119

❑ Brutalistic/Pearl White/PR5 .... $1.50

TRACK ACES 10 OF 12 120

❑ **CUL8R/M Silver/PR5** **$1.50**
❑ CUL8R/Spectraflame Red/FTE (FTE Promo) $12.00

TRACK ACES 11 OF 12 121

❑ Road Rocket/Red/5SP $3.00
❑ **Road Rocket/Red/PR5** **$1.50**

TRACK ACES   12 OF 12

❏ Sling Shot/Blue/OH5SP $1.50

HOT WHEELS

❏ Shredster/M Black & M Green/PR5............. $1.50

HOT WHEELS

❏ 'Tooned '69 Camaro Z-28/M Green/5SP .. **$3.00**
❏ 'Tooned '69 Camaro Z-28/M Purple/5SP
   (Kmart) $5.00

HOT WHEELS

❏ **'Tooned '69 Camaro Z-28/M Yellow/5SP $5.00**
❏ 'Tooned '69 Camaro Z-28/M Yellow/FTE
   (Toys R Us Starter) $12.00

HOT WHEELS

❏ 1970 Mustang Mach 1/Black/5SP $3.00

HOT WHEELS

❏ 1970 Mustang Mach 1/Blue/5SP $40.00
❏ **1970 Mustang Mach 1/Blue/7SP.............. $3.00**

HOT WHEELS

❏ Fiat 500c/M Lt. Blue/10SP, 5SP rear.......... $1.50

HOT WHEELS

❏ Tow Jam/M Lt. Blue/Y5 .... $3.00

HOT WHEELS — 2006 — 127

- ❏ Tow Jam/M Orange/Y5 .... $3.00

HOT WHEELS — 2006 — 128

- ❏ **1968 Mustang/M Copper/5SP $25.00**
- ❏ 1968 Mustang/M Copper/FTE $20.00
- ❏ 1968 Mustang/M Lt. Olive Green/
  5SP black base $3.00
- ❏ 1968 Mustang/M Lt. Olive Green/
  5SP chrome base $15.00
- ❏ 1968 Mustang/Olive Green/5SP $3.00

HOT WHEELS — 2006 — 128

- ❏ 1968 Mustang/M Orange/FTE $6.00
- ❏ **1968 Mustang/M Orange/5SP $3.00**

HOT WHEELS — 2006 — 128

- ❏ **1968 Mustang/M Pink/5SP $3.00**
- ❏ 1968 Mustang/M Pink/5SP Tam cams $3.00

HOT WHEELS — 2006 — 129

- ❏ Lotus Elise 340R/M Yellow/WSP $1.50

HOT WHEELS — 2006 — 130

- ❏ Turboa/Green/GreenPR5 .... $1.50

HOT WHEELS — 2006 — 130

- ❏ **Turboa/M Copper/GoldPR5 .... $1.50**
- ❏ Turboa/M Lt. Copper/GoldPR5 .... $1.50

HOT WHEELS — 2006 — 131

- ❏ **Mitsubishi Eclipse/M Lt. Blue/Y5 .... $1.50**
- ❏ Mitsubishi Eclipse/M Lt. Blue/Y5 5 tampos $8.00

HOT WHEELS

❏ **Pikes Peak Celica/Black/
  PR5 black interior** $1.50
❏ Pikes Peak Celica/Black/
  PR5 no tampo rear quarter $1.50
❏ Pikes Peak Celica/Black/
  PR5 orange interior.................................. $1.50

HOT WHEELS

❏ Honda Civic Type R/Black/FTE $4.00
❏ **Honda Civic Type R/Black/PR5** $1.50

HOT WHEELS

❏ Honda Civic Type R/Pearl White/PR5 .... $1.50

HOT WHEELS

❏ Twin Mill II/M Blue/5SP $3.00
❏ **Twin Mill II/M Blue/Y5** $1.50

HOT WHEELS

❏ Super Modified/M Dark Green/WSP $1.50

HOT WHEELS

❏ Super Modified/M Red/WSP $1.50

HOT WHEELS

❏ Swoop Coupe/M Purple & Grey/5SP $5.00
❏ **Swoop Coupe/M Purple & Grey/SK5,
  5SP rear** $1.50

HOT WHEELS

❏ Swoop Coupe/White & Red/SK5, 5SP rear $1.50

HOT WHEELS

❏ Swoop Coupe/Yellow & M Green/SK5, 5SP rear $1.50

HOT WHEELS

❏ Blast Lane/M Dark Red/MC3...................... $3.00

HOT WHEELS

❏ Blast Lane/Yellow/MC3 .... $3.00

HOT WHEELS

❏ Shadow Jet/M Purple/5SP.......................... $1.50

HOT WHEELS

❏ Ford GT90 Concept/M Black/3SP $1.50

HOT WHEELS

❏ L'Bling/M Dark Red/PR5 .... $1.50

HOT WHEELS

❏ Dodge Ram 1500/M Magenta/PR5 .... $1.50

HOT WHEELS

❏ Dodge Ram 1500/Orange/PR5 .... $1.50

HOT WHEELS

2006 142

- ❏ '40 Ford Truck/Flat Black/Blue5SP $1.50
- ❏ '40 Ford Truck/Grey/5SP $30.00
- ❏ **'40 Ford Truck/Grey/Blue5SP $1.50**

HOT WHEELS

2006 142

- ❏ **'40 Ford Truck/Yellow/5SP $1.50**
- ❏ '40 Ford Truck/Yellow/Y5 .... $8.00

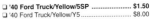

HOT WHEELS

2006 143

- ❏ Trak-Tune/Clear Green/FTE $4.00
- ❏ **Trak-Tune/Clear Green/Y5 .... $1.50**

HOT WHEELS

2006 143

- ❏ Trak-Tune/Clear Purple/Y5 .... $1.50

HOT WHEELS

2006 144

- ❏ **Bugatti Veyron/Blue-Grey/10SP $1.50**
- ❏ Bugatti Veyron/Blue-Grey/FTE $4.00

HOT WHEELS

2006 145

- ❏ Hammered Coupe/M Magenta/Gold5SP $1.50

HOT WHEELS

2006 145

- ❏ Hammered Coupe/M Red/Gold5SP $1.50

HOT WHEELS

2006 146

- ❏ Roll Cage/Lime Green/OR5SP $1.50

HOT WHEELS `2006` **147**

❑ Sharkruiser/Black/BlueY5 .... $1.50

HOT WHEELS `2006` **148**

❑ Moto-Crossed/Black/5SP....................... $40.00
❑ **Moto-Crossed/Black/PR5 .... $1.50**

HOT WHEELS `2006` **149**

❑ Ferrari 360 Modena/M Dark Red/PR5........ $1.50

HOT WHEELS `2006` **150**

❑ Deuce Roadster/M Lt. Blue/5SP $1.50

HOT WHEELS `2006` **151**

❑ Radio Flyer Wagon/Blue/5SP black spoiler $3.00
❑ **Radio Flyer Wagon/Blue/5SP chrome spoiler $1.50**

HOT WHEELS `2006` **152**

❑ Way 2 Fast/Silver/5SP............................. $3.00

HOT WHEELS `2006` **152**

❑ Way 2 Fast/Yellow/5SP $3.00

HOT WHEELS `2006` **153**

❑ Vampyra/Chrome/Gold5DOT.................... $15.00
❑ **Vampyra/Chrome/GoldWSP $3.00**

HOT WHEELS — 2006 154

- ❏ Corvette C6/Blue/PR5 (Kmart) $3.00
- ❏ Corvette C6/Blue/PR5 (Kmart) tinted windows $3.00
- ❏ **Corvette C6/White/PR5 .... $1.50**

HOT WHEELS — 2006 155

- ❏ 'Tooned 1969 Pontiac GTO/Black & Red/5SP $1.50

HOT WHEELS — 2006 156

- ❏ Vairy 8/Flat Black/5SP (Wal-Mart) $1.50
- ❏ **Vairy 8/Flat Blue/5SP................................ $1.50**

HOT WHEELS — 2006 156

- ❏ Vairy 8/Flat Dark Green/5SP $3.00

HOT WHEELS — 2006 157

- ❏ 1964 Buick Riviera/Green/WSP $1.50

HOT WHEELS — 2006 157

- ❏ 1964 Buick Riviera/Red/WSP $1.50

HOT WHEELS — 2006 158

- ❏ Fore Wheeler/Black & Red/5SP $1.50

HOT WHEELS — 2006 158

- ❏ Fore Wheeler/M Red/5SP $1.50

HOT WHEELS

2006 159

❏ 1947 Chevy Fleetline/Flat Black/WSP........ $3.00

HOT WHEELS

2006 160

❏ Itso-Skeenie/Magenta/PR5 .... $1.50

HOT WHEELS

2006 161

❏ Rocket Box/Flat Black/PR5 .... $1.50

HOT WHEELS

2006 162

❏ Torpedo Jones/Dark Red/3SP $3.00
Torpedo Jones/Dark Red/3SP silver flames $1.50
❏ Torpedo Jones/Dark Red/5SP $1.50
❏ Torpedo Jones/Dark Red/WSP $25.00

HOT WHEELS

2006 162

❏ Torpedo Jones/Dark Yellow/Gold5SP $1.50

HOT WHEELS

2006 163

❏ Toyota Celica/Black/Y5 black interior $5.00
Toyota Celica/Black/Y5 chrome interior $1.50

HOT WHEELS

2006 164

❏ Airy 8/Flat Black/RedMC3 .... $1.50

HOT WHEELS

2006 164

❏ Airy 8/Purple/MC3 .... $1.50

HOT WHEELS 2006 165

❏ Morris Cooper/Dark Red/PR5 .... $1.50

HOT WHEELS 2006 166

❏ Pikes Peak Tacoma/Pearl White/Red10SP $1.50

HOT WHEELS 2006 167

❏ **Mega-Duty/Copper/Gold5DOT $1.50**
❏ Mega-Duty/Copper/Gold5SP $25.00
❏ Mega-Duty/Copper/GoldOR5SP $3.00

HOT WHEELS 2006 168

❏ Tor-Speedo/Blue/FTE $4.00
❏ **Tor-Speedo/Blue/PR5 .... $1.50**

HOT WHEELS 2006 169

❏ Talbot Lago/M Grey/WSP $1.50

HOT WHEELS 2006 170

❏ 1941 Willys Coupe/Flat Black/
   Gold5SP black base $3.00
❏ **1941 Willys Coupe/Flat Black/Gold5SP
   gold chrome base $1.50**

HOT WHEELS 2006 171

❏ Monoposto/Silver/PR5 .... $1.50

HOT WHEELS 2006 172

❏ '69 El Camino/Grey/Gold5SP $6.00

Hot Wheels

2006 **172**
❏ '69 El Camino/Yellow/5SP (Toys R Us Starter) $6.00

Hot Wheels
2006 **173**
❏ Hummer H3T Concept/M Grey/OR5SP...... $1.50

Hot Wheels
2006 **173**
❏ Hummer H3T Concept/Yellow/OR5SP $1.50

Hot Wheels
2006 **174**
❏ Sweet 16 II/Pearl White/5SP $1.50

Hot Wheels
2006 **175**
❏ Pocket Bikester/Red/FTE $4.00
❏ **Pocket Bikester/Red/PR5 .... $1.50**

Hot Wheels
2006 **176**
❏ 1968 Dodge Dart/M Black/5SP $30.00
❏ **1968 Dodge Dart/M Black/10SP $3.00**

Hot Wheels
2006 **177**
❏ 1932 Bugatti Type 50/M Green/Gold5DOT $1.50

Hot Wheels
2006 **178**
❏ Arachnorod/Grey/PR5 .... $1.50

HOT WHEELS 2006 **179**
❏ Jester/Black/BluePR5 .... $1.50

HOT WHEELS 2006 **180**
❏ Saleen S7/Dark Blue/PR5 .... $1.50

HOT WHEELS 2006 **181**
❏ 1963 Thunderbird/Pearl White/WSP $1.50

HOT WHEELS 2006 **182**
❏ 1968 Mercury Cougar/M Green/5SP $1.50

HOT WHEELS 2006 **182**
❏ 1968 Mercury Cougar/Orange/5SP $1.50

HOT WHEELS 2006 **183**
❏ Scorchin' Scooter/M Green/MC3 .... $3.00

HOT WHEELS 2006 **183**
❏ Scorchin' Scooter/M Purple/GoldMC3
   black handlebars $3.00
❏ Scorchin' Scooter/M Purple/GoldMC3
   grey handlebars $10.00

HOT WHEELS 2006 **184**
❏ **2005 Ford Mustang GT/M Grey/PR5** $25.00
❏ **2005 Ford Mustang GT/M Grey/Y5** $1.50

HOT WHEELS

2006 184

❑ 2005 Ford Mustang GT/Yellow/PR5 .... $1.50

HOT WHEELS
2006 185

❑ Flight '03/M Gold/5SP $10.00
❑ Flight '03/M Gold/10SP $1.50
❑ Flight '03/M Gold/PR5 .... $10.00

HOT WHEELS

2006 186

❑ Altered State/Black/5SP $1.50

HOT WHEELS
2006 187

❑ Wild Thing/Dark Red/Mini $1.50

HOT WHEELS

2006 188

❑ Sinistra/Black/GoldPR5 .... $1.50

HOT WHEELS
2006 189

❑ Oscar Mayer Wienermobile/
 Yellow & Red/Gold5SP $1.50

HOT WHEELS

2006 190

❑ 3-Window '34/Flat Black/5SP $1.50
❑ 3-Window '34/Grey/5SP $1.50

HOT WHEELS
2006 191

❑ Old Number 5.5/Red/5SP $1.50
❑ Old Number 5.5/Red/OH5SP $3.00
❑ Old Number 5.5/Yellow/5SP $1.50

HOT WHEELS

❏ Lotus Project M250/Green/5SP $1.50

HOT WHEELS

❏ **Invader/Tan/Black5SP $1.50**
❏ Invader/Tan/BlackPR5 .... $8.00

HOT WHEELS

❏ Enzo Ferrari/Black/GoldOH5SP $1.50

HOT WHEELS

❏ Ferrari 333SP/Black/5SP $1.50

HOT WHEELS

❏ Shock Factor/Salmon Red/OR5SP $1.50

HOT WHEELS

❏ VW Bug/Black/5SP (Wal-Mart Red) $30.00
❏ **VW Bug/Black/GoldY5 .... $1.50**
❏ VW Bug/White/5SP (Wal-Mart) $3.00

HOT WHEELS

❏ Hot Bird/Black/5SP $10.00
❏ **Hot Bird/Black/7SP $1.50**
❏ Hot Bird/M Purple/5SP $1.50

HOT WHEELS

❏ Acura HSC Concept/M Red/5SP $1.50

HOT WHEELS 2006 200

❏ Ford F-150/M Red/OR5SP $1.50

HOT WHEELS 2006 201

❏ Ferrari 575 GTC/Grey/PR5 .... $1.50

HOT WHEELS 2006 202

❏ I Candy/M Green/PR5 .... $1.50

HOT WHEELS 2006 203

❏ Ground FX/M Green/BlackSK5 .... $3.00
❏ **Ground FX/M Green/SK5 .... $1.50**

HOT WHEELS 2006 204

❏ Hyper Mite/M Silver & Blue/5SP $1.50

HOT WHEELS 2006 205

❏ Vulture Roadster/Black/OH5SP.................. $1.50

HOT WHEELS 2006 206

❏ **Ford Shelby GR-1 Concept/Flat Black/PR5 $1.50**
❏ Ford Shelby GR-1 Concept/M Dark Red/PR5 $1.50

HOT WHEELS 2006 207

❏ Batmobile/Flat Black/GoldPR5 .... $1.50

HOT WHEELS

❏ **GMC Motorhome/Black/5SP** **$3.00**
❏ GMC Motorhome/Black/PR5 .... $15.00
❏ GMC Motorhome/White/5SP (Kmart) $60.00
❏ GMC Motorhome/White/PR5 (Kmart) $5.00

HOT WHEELS

❏ **MS-T Suzuka/Orange/Blue10SP** **$1.50**
❏ MS-T Suzuka/Orange/BluePR5.................. $1.50

HOT WHEELS

❏ 8 Crate/Dark Blue/5SP $3.00

HOT WHEELS

❏ Nomadder What/M Yellow/5SP $1.50
❏ **Nomadder What/M Yellow/PR5**................ **$1.50**

HOT WHEELS

❏ Shelby Cobra 427 S/C/M Gray/5SP $1.50

HOT WHEELS

❏ Greased Lightnin'/Black/GoldPR5 .... $1.50

HOT WHEELS

❏ Poison Arrow/Smoke Tinted/Micro5SP $1.50

HOT WHEELS

❏ Double Vision/Pearl White/PR5.................. $1.50

HOT WHEELS 2006 216
❑ Overbored 454/Black/PR5 .... $1.50

HOT WHEELS 2006 217
❑ Slideout/M Blue/PR5 .... $1.50

HOT WHEELS 2006 218
❑ 'Tooned Mercy Breaker/Dark Blue/PR5 ...... $1.50

2006 MYSTERY CAR 1 OF 5 2006 219
❑ Dairy Delivery/Dark Blue/WLRR $25.00

2006 MYSTERY CAR 2 OF 5 2006 220
❑ '70 Chevelle/M Orange/RLRR5SP $25.00

2006 MYSTERY CAR 3 OF 5 2006 221
❑ Airy 8/Yellow/GoldMC3 .... $15.00

2006 MYSTERY CAR 4 OF 5 2006 222
❑ '55 Chevy Panel/M Purple/RLRR5SP $30.00

2006 MYSTERY CAR 5 OF 5 2006 223
❑ Customized VW Drag Bus/Chrome & Black/RR5SP
(10th Anniversary) $50.00

Hot Wheels Logo

Segment Vehicle Number

2007 NEW MODELS

Segment Name

Vehicle Name

Blister

2007

❑ **Dodge Challenger Concept/Green/5SP .. $3.00**
❑ Dodge Challenger Concept/Green/PR5 .... $1.50

❑ Dodge Challenger Concept/M Dark Red/PR5 $1.50

❑ Dodge Challenger Concept/M Grey/PR5 .. $1.50

❑ Dodge Challenger Concept/M Orange/PR5 $1.50

2007 NEW MODELS — 2 OF 36 — 002

❑ Chevy Camaro Concept/Black/OH5SP $1.50

2007 NEW MODELS — 2 OF 36 — 002

❑ Chevy Camaro Concept/M Orange/
OH5SP (K-Mart) $5.00

2007 NEW MODELS — 2 OF 36 — 002

❑ **Chevy Camaro Concept/M Silver/
OH5SP black base** **$1.50**
❑ Chevy Camaro Concept/M Silver/
OH5SP chrome base $1.50

2007 NEW MODELS — 2 OF 36 — 002

❑ Chevy Camaro Concept/Red/5SP.............. $5.00
❑ **Chevy Camaro Concept/Red/OH5SP** **$1.50**

2007 NEW MODELS — 3 OF 36 — 003

❑ Nitro Doorslammer/M Burgundy/GoldOH5SP $1.50

2007 NEW MODELS — 3 OF 36 — 003

❑ Nitro Doorslammer/M Gold/RedOH5SP $1.50

2007 NEW MODELS — 4 OF 36 — 004

❑ **'69 Ford Mustang/Black/OH5SP** **$1.50**
❑ '69 Ford Mustang/Black/PR5...................... $5.00

2007 NEW MODELS — 4 OF 36 — 004

❑ '69 Ford Mustang/M Dark Red/5SP $1.50
❑ **'69 Ford Mustang/M Dark Red/OH5SP** **$1.50**

❑ '69 Ford Mustang/M Dark Yellow/OH5SP .. $1.50

❑ '69 Ford Mustang/Pearl White/OH5SP $1.50
❑ '69 Ford Mustang/Pearl White/PR5 .... $5.00

❑ Dodge Ram 1500/Black/OR5SP $3.00

❑ Dodge Ram 1500/M Dark Purple/OR5SP .. $3.00

❑ Dodge Ram 1500/M Dark Red/OR5SP...... $3.00

❑ Dodge Ram 1500/Pearl Yellow/OR5SP (K-Mart) $3.00

❑ Shelby Cobra Daytona Coupe/M Dark Blue/OH5SP... $1.50

❑ Shelby Cobra Daytona Coupe/
   M Silver/PR5 large 59 .... $1.50
❑ Shelby Cobra Daytona Coupe/
   M Silver/PR5 small 59 .... $3.00

❑ Shelby Cobra Daytona Coupe/M Teal/OH5SP $1.50

❑ **Shelby Cobra Daytona Coupe/Red/OH5SP $1.50**
❑ Shelby Cobra Daytona Coupe/Red/PR5 .... $3.00

❑ Dodge Charger SRT8/M Orange/Y5 .... $1.50

❑ Dodge Charger SRT8/M Red-Orange/
    Y5 orange spoiler $1.50
❑ Dodge Charger SRT8/M Red-Orange/
    Y5 red spoiler $5.00

❑ Dodge Charger SRT8/M Silver/Y5 .... $1.50

❑ Dodge Charger SRT8/M Yellow/Y5 .... $1.50

❑ Rogue Hog/Black/BlackOH5SP $1.50

❑ '66 Chevy Nova/Champagne/PR5 .... $1.50

❏ '66 Chevy Nova/Flat Black/
5SP black base $3.00
❏ '66 Chevy Nova/Flat Black/
5SP chrome base $1.50

❏ '66 Chevy Nova/M Blue/PR5 .... $1.50

❏ '66 Chevy Nova/Pearl White/5SP $3.00

❏ Buick Grand National/Black/5SP $15.00
❏ **Buick Grand National/Black/OH5SP** **$1.50**

❏ Buick Grand National/M Blue/OH5SP (K-Mart) $20.00

❏ Buick Grand National/M Burgundy/5SP $1.50

❏ **Buick Grand National/Silver/**
10SP black interior **$1.50**
❏ Buick Grand National/Silver/
10SP chrome interior $25.00
❏ Buick Grand National/Silver/
Y5 chrome inetrior $12.00
❏ Buick Grand National/Silver/
Y5 black interior $125.00

❏ Wastelander/Black/BlackORMC $3.00
❏ **Wastelander/Black/GoldORMC** **$1.50**

❏ Wastelander/Dark Olive Green/ORMC $1.50

❏ Wastelander/Grey/RedORMC $1.50

❏ Wastelander/M Red/ORMC $1.50

❏ Straight Pipes/Black/5SP black interior $30.00
❏ **Straight Pipes/Black/5SP red interior $1.50**

❏ Straight Pipes/M Red/5SP $1.50

❏ Straight Pipes/M Silver/5SP $1.50

❏ Straight Pipes/Yellow/5SP $1.50

❏ Sky Knife/Antifreeze Green/Micro5SP........ $1.50

2007 **013**

❑ Sky Knife/Blue/Micro5SP............................ $1.50

2007 **013**

❑ Sky Knife/M Red/Micro5SP $1.50

  2007 **014**

❑ Ferrari 599 GTB/Black/PR5........................ $1.50

 2007 **014**

❑ **Ferrari 599 GTB/Red/PR5 .... $1.50**
❑ Ferrari 599 GTB/Red/PR5 orange headlights $1.50

  2007 **014**

❑ Ferrari 599 GTB/Yellow/PR5 .... $1.50

 2007 **015**

❑ '66 Batmobile/Black/5SP $5.00
❑ '66 Batmobile/Black/5DOT...................... $200.00

  2007 **016**

❑ **'70 Pontiac Firebird/M Blue/PR5.............. $1.50**
❑ '70 Pontiac Firebird/M Blue/PR5 scum bum $5.00

 2007 **016**

❑ '70 Pontiac Firebird/M Gold/PR5 .... $1.50

2007

❏ '70 Pontiac Firebird/M Silver/PR5 (K-Mart) $5.00

❏ '70 Pontiac Firebird/Pearl White/PR5 .... $1.50

❏ Ford GTX1/Blue/5SP.............................. $15.00
❏ **Ford GTX1/Blue/OH5SP $1.50**
❏ Ford GTX1/Blue/PR5................................ $1.50

❏ Ford GTX1/M Dark Yellow/OH5SP $1.50

❏ **Ford GTX1/Pearl White/5SP $1.50**
❏ Ford GTX1/Pearl White/OH5SP $30.00

❏ 1964 Ford Galaxie 500XL/M Blue/5SP $1.50

❏ 1964 Ford Galaxie 500XL/M Dark Red/5SP $3.00

❏ 1964 Ford Galaxie 500XL/M Powder Blue/5SP $1.50

❏ 1964 Ford Galaxie 500XL/
Pearl White/5SP (K-Mart) $5.00

❏ CCM Country Club Muscle/Champagne/PR5 $1.50

❏ Chevy Silverado/M Black/OH5SP $3.00

❏ Chevy Silverado/M Blue/OH5SP $1.50

❏ Chevy Silverado/M Dark Orange/OH5SP .. $3.00

❏ Chevy Silverado/M Dark Red/OH5SP $3.00

❏ Nitro Scorcher/M Blue/OH5SP $3.00

❏ Nitro Scorcher/M Silver/OH5SP $1.50
❏ Nitro Scorcher/Red/OH5SP $1.50
❏ Nitro Scorcher/Red/
    OH5SP ferracin' base $1.50
❏ (Nitro Scorcher)/Red/
    OH5SP nitro base $1.50

2007

❏ '64 Lincoln Continental/
M Dark Blue/White5SP $20.00
❏ '64 Lincoln Continental/M Dark Blue/
WhiteOH5SP $1.50

❏ '64 Lincoln Continental/
M Dark Purple/WSP............................... $1.50
❏ '64 Lincoln Continental/
Pearl White/GoldOH5SP......................... $1.50
❏ '64 Lincoln Continental/Silver/White5SP $200.00

❏ Ferrari 250 LM/Powder Blue/10SP $1.50

❏ Ferrari 250 LM/Red/WSP $1.50

❏ Ferrari 250 LM/Yellow/WSP black base $3.00
❏ Ferrari 250 LM/Yellow/WSP chrome base $1.50

❏ Supdogg/M Brown/GoldOH5SP $1.50

❏ Solar Reflex/Gold Chrome/Y5 .... $1.50

❏ Buzz Bomb/Black/OH5SP $1.50

2007 027

❏ Volkswagen Golf GTI/M Blue/Y5 black base $1.50
❏ **Volkswagen Golf GTI/M Blue/**
Y5 chrome base $1.50

2007 027

❏ Volkswagen Golf GTI/
M Dark Orange/CopperY5 (K-Mart).............. $5.00

2007 027

❏ Volkswagen Golf GTI/Pearl White/Y5 .... $1.50

2007 028

❏ Drift King/M Gold/RedOH5SP $1.50

2007 028

❏ Drift King/M Lt. Green/RedOH5SP $1.50

2007 029

❏ Jet Threat 4.0/M Black/10SP...................... $3.00
❏ Jet Threat 4.0/M Black/5SP........................ $1.50
❏ **Jet Threat 4.0/M Black/OH5SP** $1.50

2007 029

❏ Jet Threat 4.0/M Silver/CopperOH5SP $1.50

2007 029

❏ Jet Threat 4.0/Red/10SP $1.50

2007 New Models — 30 of 36

❑ Cloak And Dagger/Black Clear w/Green/OH5SP $1.50

2007 New Models — 30 of 36

❑ Cloak And Dagger/
Red Clear w/Blue/OH5SP (K-Mart) $5.00

2007 New Models — 31 of 36

❑ Ultra Rage/Red/OH5SP $1.50

2007 New Models — 32 of 36

❑ Porsche Cayman S/M Red/OH5SP $1.50

2007 New Models — 32 of 36

❑ Porsche Cayman S/M Silver/OH5SP $1.50

2007 New Models — 32 of 36

❑ Porsche Cayman S/Pearl Yellow/OH5SP .. $1.50

2007 New Models — 33 of 36

❑ Fast Fortress/Flat Grey/5SP $1.50
❑ **Fast Fortress/Flat Grey/OH5SP $1.50**

2007 New Models — 33 of 36

❑ Fast Fortress/Olive Green/5SP $1.50

❏ Custom '53 Chevy/M Copper/5SP (K-Mart) $5.00

❏ Custom '53 Chevy/M Dark Red/5SP $3.00

❏ Custom '53 Chevy/M Purple/5SP $3.00

❏ Shell Shock/M Red/RedOH5SP $1.50

❏ Split Vision/Pearl Yellow/OH5SP $1.50

❏ Morris Mini/Pearl White/10SP $3.00

❏ Hyperliner/Flat Black/BlackOH5SP $1.50

❏ Volkswagen New Beetle Cup/
   M Teal/10SP $3.00
❏ **Volkswagen New Beetle Cup/**
   M Teal/Yellow10SP.................................. $3.00

HOT WHEELS

POP-OFFS 4 OF 4

❏ Ground FX/M Purple/SK5 .... $1.50

CAMARO 1 OF 4

❏ '69 Camaro Conv./M Dark Red/
  5SP chrome Malaysia base $3.00
❏ **'69 Camaro Conv./**
  M Dark Red/5SP chrome Thailand base **$3.00**
❏ '69 Camaro Conv./M Dark Red/
  PR5 black Malaysia base $3.00
❏ '69 Camaro Conv./M Dark Red/
  PR5 chrome Malaysia base $3.00
❏ '69 Camaro Conv./M Dark Red/
  PR5 chrome Thailand base............................ $3.00

CAMARO 2 OF 4

❏ **'67 Camaro/M Dark Blue/5SP** **$3.00**
❏ '67 Camaro/M Dark Blue/PR5 .... $8.00

CAMARO 3 OF 4

❏ Camaro Z28/M Grey/5SP $1.50
❏ Camaro Z28/M Grey/Y5 .... $3.00
❏ Camaro Z28/M Grey/Y5
  black Malaysia base $3.00

CAMARO 4 OF 4

❏ Camaro Z28/M Yellow/PR5 .... $1.50

HOT WHEELS DESIGN 1 OF 4

❏ Pony-Up/M Dark Orange/PR5 .... $1.50

HOT WHEELS DESIGN 2 OF 4

❏ Hyper Mite/Dark Olive Green/5SP $1.50

HOT WHEELS DESIGN 3 OF 4

❏ Asphalt Assault/M Green/10SP $1.50

2007
040
041
042
043
044
045
046
046

HOT WHEELS DESIGN   4 OF 4

❏ CUL8R/Pearl Yellow/GoldOH5SP $1.50
❏ CUL8R/Pearl Yellow/GoldPR5 .... $1.50

TAXI RODS   1 OF 4

❏ Cockney Cab II/M Gold/5SP $1.50

TAXI RODS   2 OF 4

❏ '55 Chevy/Yellow/5SP $3.00

TAXI RODS   3 OF 4

❏ '70 Plymouth Road Runner/
   M Black/5SP black TAXI $3.00
❏ **'70 Plymouth Road Runner/
   M Black/5SP grey TAXI** **$3.00**
❏ '70 Plymouth Road Runner/
   M Black/OH5SP $3.00

TAXI RODS   4 OF 4

❏ **1964 Chevy Impala/M Yellow/
   GoldWSP clear windows** **$1.50**
❏ 1964 Chevy Impala/M Yellow/
   GoldWSP tinted windows $3.00

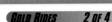

GOLD RIDES   1 OF 4

❏ Chrysler 300C/Gold Chrome/GoldBLING .. $1.50

GOLD RIDES   2 OF 4

❏ '07 Cadillac Escalade/Gold Chrome/GoldPR5 $1.50

GOLD RIDES   3 OF 4

❏ Humvee/Gold Chrome/GoldOR5SP $1.50

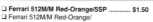

GOLD RIDES   4 OF 4

❑ Unobtainium 1/Gold Chrome/GoldBLING .. $1.50

ENGINE REVEALERS   1 OF 4

❑ Ferrari 512M/M Red-Orange/5SP $1.50
❑ Ferrari 512M/M Red-Orange/
   PR5 Malaysia base $1.50
❑ Ferrari 512M/M Red-Orange/
   PR5 Thailand base $1.50

ENGINE REVEALERS   2 OF 4

❑ 1969 Dodge Charger/Pearl White/
   5SP Malaysia Base $3.00
❑ **1969 Dodge Charger/Pearl White/**
   5SP Thailand Base **$3.00**

ENGINE REVEALERS   3 OF 4

❑ '58 Corvette/M Dark Grey/5SP $1.50

ENGINE REVEALERS   4 OF 4

❑ Tire Fryer/Black/OH5SP $3.00
❑ **Tire Fryer/Black/SK5 front, 5SP rear ......** **$1.50**

HUMMER   1 OF 4

❑ Hummer H2/Champagne/
   OR5SP Malaysia base $1.50
❑ **Hummer H2/Champagne/**
   OR5SP Thailand base **$1.50**

HUMMER   2 OF 4

❑ Hummer H3T Concept/M Dark Blue/OR5SP $1.50

HUMMER   3 OF 4

❑ Hummer H3/Red/
   GoldOH5SP Malaysia base $1.50
❑ **Hummer H3/Red/**
   GoldOH5SP Thailand base **$1.50**

❑ Hummer H2/M Grey/BLING.................. $1.50

❑ Preying Menace/Black/PR5...................... $1.50

❑ Sharkruiser/Grey/3SP $1.50

❑ Arachnorod/Blue-Grey/
     5SP Malaysia base $8.00
❑ Arachnorod/Blue-Grey/
     5SP Thailand base $8.00
❑ Arachnorod/Blue-Grey/
     OH5SP Malaysia base $1.50
❑ **Arachnorod/Blue-Grey/**
     OH5SP Thailand base $1.50

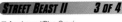

❑ Rodzilla/Purple/GoldPR5.......................... $1.50

❑ Nerve Hammer/Clear/3SP $1.50

❑ Stockar/Clear/BluePR5 .... $1.50

❑ Phastasm/Clear/GreenOH5SP $12.00
❑ **Phastasm/Clear/GreenPR5 .... $1.50**

X-Raygers 4 OF 4

❏ Vandetta/Clear/RedPR5 .... $1.50

AERIAL ATTACK 1 OF 4

❏ Mad Propz/M Orange/Micro5SP $1.50

AERIAL ATTACK 2 OF 4

❏ Killer Copter/Olive Green............................ $3.00

AERIAL ATTACK 3 OF 4

❏ Poison Arrow/Clear Red/GoldMicro5SP $1.50

AERIAL ATTACK 4 OF 4

❏ Blimp/Silver $1.50

HOT WHEELS RACING 1 OF 4

❏ 1941 Willys Coupe/M Dark Blue/5SP $1.50

HOT WHEELS RACING 2 OF 4

❏ 24/Seven/M Dark Blue/OH5SP $1.50

HOT WHEELS RACING 3 OF 4

❏ Formul8r/M Dark Blue/White10SP $1.50

☐ Datsun 240Z/M Dark Blue/Y5 .... $1.50

☐ Tantrum/M Dark Red/3SP $1.50

☐ '33 Ford/Black/SK5 front, 3SP rear **$1.50**
☐ '33 Ford/Black/SK5 front, 5SP rear $1.50

☐ '70 Chevelle (Convertible)/M Orange/RL5SP $3.00

☐ Mitsubishi Eclipse/M Black/5SP $8.00
☐ **Mitsubishi Eclipse/M Black/Y5** **$1.50**

☐ Dodge Charger Daytona/M Blue/5SP $1.50

☐ Dodge Charger Daytona/M Green/5SP...... $1.50

☐ Cadillac Cien Concept/M Blue/PR5............ $1.50

CODE CAR 3 OF 24

❑ Muscle Tone/M Gold/OH5SP...................... $1.50

CODE CAR 3 OF 24

❑ Muscle Tone/M Red/RedPR5 .... $1.50

CODE CAR 4 OF 24

❑ Audacious/Black/Y5.................................. $1.50

CODE CAR 4 OF 24

❑ Audacious/M Dark Red/GoldPR5 .... $8.00
❑ **Audacious/M Dark Red/GoldY5 .... $1.50**

CODE CAR 5 OF 24

❑ Overbored 454/Black/PR5.......................... $1.50

CODE CAR 5 OF 24

❑ Overbored 454/M Silver/PR5...................... $1.50

CODE CAR 6 OF 24

❑ Rocket Box/M Purple/PR5........................ $1.50

CODE CAR 6 OF 24

❑ Rocket Box/Yellow/PR5.............................. $1.50

☐ **Monoposto/M Dark Green/5DOT** **$1.50**
☐ Monoposto/M Dark Green/Y5 .... $3.00

☐ Aston Martin V8 Vantage/M Red/PR5 .... $1.50

☐ Aston Martin V8 Vantage/M Silver/PR5...... $1.50

☐ I Candy/Dark Blue/BluePR5 .... $1.50

☐ Lotus Esprit/Black/Y5 .... $1.50

☐ Lotus Esprit/M Silver/Y5 .... $1.50

☐ Toyota RSC/M Dark Orange/OR5SP $1.50

☐ Toyota RSC/Pearl Lt. Blue/OR5SP $1.50

2007

CODE CAR *12 OF 24*   2007 **096**

❑ Xtreemster/M Gold/PR5 .... $1.50

CODE CAR *13 OF 24*   2007 **097**

❑ Shelby Cobra 427 S/C/M Dark Blue/10SP $1.50

CODE CAR *13 OF 24*   2007 **097**

❑ **Shelby Cobra 427 S/C/M Magenta/10SP $1.50**
❑ Shelby Cobra 427 S/C/M Magenta/WSP .. $1.50

CODE CAR *14 OF 24*   2007 **098**

❑ Dodge Power Wagon/M Green/OR5SP $1.50

CODE CAR *14 OF 24*   2007 **098**

❑ Dodge Power Wagon/M Red/OR5SP $1.50

CODE CAR *15 OF 24*   2007 **099**

❑ Whip Creamer II/M Dark Purple/GreyOH5SP $1.50

CODE CAR *15 OF 24*   2007 **099**

❑ Whip Creamer II/M Gold/Red5SP $1.50

CODE CAR *16 OF 24*   2007 **100**

❑ Honda Civic Si/M Blue/Y5 .... $1.50

2007 100

❏ **Honda Civic Si/M Red/10SP** $1.50
❏ Honda Civic Si/M Red/OH5SP $1.50

2007 101

❏ AMG-Mercedes CLK DTM/M Dark Red/OH5SP $1.50

2007 101

❏ AMG-Mercedes CLK DTM/M Silver/PR5 .. $1.50

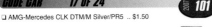

2007 102

❏ **Suzuki GSX-R/4/M Copper/5DOT** $1.50
❏ Suzuki GSX-R/4/M Copper/OrangeOH5SP $15.00

2007 103

❏ Dieselboy/M Blue/OH5SP $1.50

2007 103

❏ Dieselboy/M Copper/OH5SP $1.50

2007 104

❏ '68 Cougar/Black/5SP $1.50

2007 104

❏ '68 Cougar/M Green/5SP $1.50

2007

❏ Motoblade/M Green/OH5SP $1.50

❏ Motoblade/M Red/OH5SP $1.50

❏ Custom Cougar/M Dark Orange/OrangePR5 $1.50

❏ **So Fine/M Gold/5SP**................................. **$1.50**
❏ So Fine/M Gold/Y5 .... $3.00

❏ So Fine/Red/5SP $1.50

❏ Mitsubishi Eclipse Concept/
   M Blue/Gold10SP $1.50

❏ Pharodox/Clear Red/GoldOH5SP $1.50

❏ **Subaru Impreza/Black/10SP** **$1.50**
❏ Subaru Impreza/Black/PR5 .... $8.00

2007   **110**

❑ **Subaru Impreza/White/10SP** **$1.50**
❑ Subaru Impreza/White/PR5 .... $8.00

2007   **111**

❑ Split Decision/Flat Black/BlueOH5SP $1.50

2007   **111**

❑ Split Decision/Red/GoldY5 .... $1.50

2007   **112**

❑ Backdraft/Magenta/PR5 .... $1.50

2007   **113**

❑ Flathead Fury/Blue/GoldOH5SP $1.50

2007   **113**

❑ **Flathead Fury/Chrome/OH5SP** **$1.50**
❑ Flathead Fury/Chrome/PR5 .... $8.00

2007   **114**

❑ Rivited/Dark Orange/PR5 .... $1.50

2007   **115**

❑ Iridium/Dark Red/OH5SP $1.50

2007

TRACK STARS 7 OF 12 — 2007 — 115

❏ Iridium/M Blue/5SP $1.50
❏ **Iridium/M Blue/OH5SP**........................... **$1.50**
❏ Iridium/M Blue/PR5 .... $1.50

TRACK STARS 8 OF 12 — 2007 — 116

❏ Bassline/Black/5SP $1.50
❏ **Bassline/Black/OH5SP** **$1.50**

TRACK STARS 8 OF 12 — 2007 — 116

❏ Bassline/Blue/OH5SP $1.50

TRACK STARS 9 OF 12 — 2007 — 117

❏ Anthracite/Orange/Gold10SP $1.50

TRACK STARS 10 OF 12 — 2007 — 118

❏ Spectyte/Green/PR5 .... $1.50

TRACK STARS 11 OF 12 — 2007 — 119

❏ Piledriver/Beige/OH5SP $1.50

TRACK STARS 12 OF 12 — 2007 — 120

❏ Hollowback/M Grey/10SP $1.50

TREASURE HUNTS 1 OF 12 — 2007 — 121

❏ '69 Pontiac GTO/Dark Blue & Yellow/5SP $10.00

❏ '69 Pontiac GTO/M Spectraflame Blue & Yellow
/RR5SP...$40.00

❏ Nissan Skyline/M Dark Orange/PR5 .... $8.00

❏ Nissan Skyline/Spectraflame Copper/6SPBLING ... $20.00

❏ '69 Camaro Z28/Green/5SP $12.00

❏ '69 Camaro Z28/M Spectraflame Green/RR5SP $40.00

❏ Corvette C6R/Black/Gold10SP $12.00

❏ Corvette C6R/Black/Gold6SPBLING........ $30.00

❏ Corvette C6R/Dark Grey/
   Gold6SPBLING (Toys-R-Us)................... $40.00

2007

TREASURE HUNTS — 5 OF 12 — 2007 — 125
❑ Mega Thrust/Orange/OH5SP $8.00

TREA$URE HUNT$ — 5 OF 12 — 2007 — 125
❑ Mega Thrust/Spectraflame Dark Orange/RR5SP $25.00

TREASURE HUNTS — 6 OF 12 — 2007 — 126
❑ Hammer Sled/Yellow/MC5 .... $8.00

TREA$URE HUNT$ — 6 OF 12 — 2007 — 126
❑ Hammer Sled/Spectraflame Antifreeze/
    YellowMC5 .... $30.00

TREASURE HUNTS — 7 OF 12 — 2007 — 127
❑ Brutalistic/Dark Olive Green/WW5SP $6.00

TREA$URE HUNT$ — 7 OF 12 — 2007 — 127
❑ Brutalistic/Spectraflame Olive/RR5SP...... $25.00

TREASURE HUNTS — 8 OF 12 — 2007 — 128
❑ Jaded/M Blue/5SP $6.00

TREA$URE HUNT$ — 8 OF 12 — 2007 — 128
❑ Jaded/Spectraflame Blue/RR5SP $30.00

❏ Enzo Ferrari/Red/PR5 black seats $10.00
❏ Enzo Ferrari/Red/PR5 red seats............. $6.00

❏ Enzo Ferrari/Spectraflame Red/6SPBLING $50.00

❏ Custom '69 Chevy/M Gold/PR5.................. $8.00

❏ Custom '69 Chevy/
    Spectraflame Gold/6SPBLING $30.00

❏ Cadillac V16/Pearl Pink/OH5SP $15.00

❏ Cadillac V16/Spectraflame Pink/WWRR5SP $40.00

❏ Evil Twin/Red/OH5SP $8.00
❏ Evil Twin/Red no flames/OH5SP $25.00

❏ Evil Twin/Spectraflame Red/WWRR6SP .. $20.00

2007

2007 ALL STARS
133

❏ Slideout/Black/PR5's (K-Mart) $3.00

2007 ALL STARS
133

❏ Slideout/M Dark Red/PR5 .... $1.50

2007 ALL STARS
133

❏ Slideout/White/PR5 .... $1.50

2007 ALL STARS
134

❏ Ford GT-40/M Dark Grey/5SP $1.50

2007 ALL STARS
134

❏ Ford GT-40/M Red/5SP $1.50

2007 ALL STARS
135

❏ Go Kart/Antifreeze Micro Yellow/5DOT (Wal-Mart) $5.00

2007 ALL STARS
135

❏ **Go Kart/M Blue/5DOT** **$3.00**
❏ Go Kart/M Blue/5SP $3.00

2007 ALL STARS
136

❏ Deuce Roadster/Flat Black/Gold5SP $1.50

2007 ALL STARS
 2007 136

❑ Deuce Roadster/Flat Brown/Gold5SP $1.50

2007 ALL STARS
2007 136

❑ Deuce Roadster/Olive Green/Gold5SP $1.50

2007 ALL STARS
2007 137

❑ 1967 Pontiac GTO/Black/5SP $3.00

2007 ALL STARS
2007 137

❑ 1967 Pontiac GTO/M Red/5SP $3.00

2007 ALL STARS
2007 137

❑ 1967 Pontiac GTO/M Teal/5SP $3.00

2007 ALL STARS
2007 138

❑ Blast Lane/M Dark Blue/MC3 .... $3.00

2007 ALL STARS
2007 138

❑ Blast Lane/M Dark Purple/MC3 .... $3.00

2007 ALL STARS
2007 138

❑ Blast Lane/M Lt. Blue/MC3 (K-Mart) $6.00

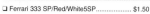

2007 All Stars — 2007 139

❏ Ferrari 333 SP/Flat Black/5SP $1.50

2007 All Stars — 2007 139

❏ Ferrari 333 SP/Red/White5SP $1.50

2007 All Stars — 2007 139

❏ Ferrari 333 SP/Yellow/White5SP $1.50

2007 All Stars — 2007 140

❏ 1964 Buick Riviera/M Gold/10SP $1.50

2007 All Stars — 2007 140

❏ 1964 Buick Riviera/M Grey/10SP (Wal-Mart) $3.00

2007 All Stars — 2007 140

❏ 1964 Buick Riviera/M Purple/10SP $1.50

2007 All Stars — 2007 141

❏ Shift Kicker/Flat Black\
    RedSK5 front Red5SP rear $1.50

2007 All Stars — 2007 141

❏ Shift Kicker/Flat Grey/
    BlackSK5 front, Black5SP rear $1.50

2007 ALL STARS 2007 **141**

❏ Shift Kicker/M Red/
   SK5 front, 5SP rear (Wal-Mart)................ $3.00

2007 ALL STARS 2007 **142**

❏ Invader/M Grey/Black5SP $1.50

2007 ALL STARS 2007 **142**

❏ Invader/Olive Green/Black5SP $1.50

2007 ALL STARS 2007 **143**

❏ Ford Thunderbolt/Flat Black/5SP $3.00
❏ **Ford Thunderbolt/Flat Black/PR5 .... $1.50**

2007 ALL STARS 2007 **143**

❏ **Ford Thunderbolt/Pearl White/**
   White 5SP silver base.............................. $1.50
❏ Ford Thunderbolt/Pearl White/
   White 5SP white base $10.00

2007 ALL STARS 2007 **143**

❏ Ford Thunderbolt/Yellow/
   Red5SP black base $12.00
❏ **Ford Thunderbolt/Yellow/**
   Red5SP chrome base $1.50
❏ Ford Thunderbolt/Yellow/
   Red5SP grey base $8.00

2007 ALL STARS 2007 **144**

❏ Pontiac Firebird/M Dark Grey/5DOT $5.00
❏ **Pontiac Firebird/M Dark Grey/5SP $1.50**

2007 ALL STARS 2007 **144**

❏ Pontiac Firebird/M Dark Red/OH5SP $1.50

2007 All Stars

❏ **Pontiac Firebird/M Lt. Blue/OH5SP** **$1.50**
❏ **Pontiac Firebird/M Lt. Blue/Y5**................... **$1.50**

2007 All Stars

❏ Mo' Scoot/Grey/Black SCR $1.50

2007 All Stars

❏ Porsche 911 GT3 Cup/
  Black/10SP (Wal-Mart) $8.00
❏ **Porsche 911 GT3 Cup/**
  Black/PR5 (Wal-Mart) **$1.50**

2007 All Stars

❏ Porsche 911 GT3 Cup/M Dark Red/PR5.... $1.50

2007 All Stars

❏ Whatta Drag/Black/SK5............................. $1.50

2007 All Stars

❏ Whatta Drag/Yellow/5SP $1.50

2007 All Stars

❏ Ferrari F50/Red/PR5 .... $1.50

2007 All Stars

❏ Shredded/Yellow & M Silver/OrangePR5 .. $1.50

2007 ALL STARS — 150

❑ '63 Corvette/Dark Blue/10SP....................... $1.50

2007 ALL STARS — 150

❑ '63 Corvette/Pearl White/10SP $1.50

2007 ALL STARS — 151

❑ Custom '59 Cadillac/Flat Black/WSP (K-Mart) $5.00

2007 ALL STARS — 151

❑ Custom '59 Cadillac/M Dark Blue/WSP $3.00

2007 ALL STARS — 152

❑ Nissan Z/M Gold/GoldOH5SP Malaysia base $1.50
❑ Nissan Z/M Gold/GoldOH5SP Thailand base $1.50
❑ **Nissan Z/M Gold/GoldPR5 .... $1.50**

2007 ALL STARS — 152

❑ Nissan Z/M Silver/PR5 .... $1.50

2007 ALL STARS — 153

❑ Purple Passion/M Silver/Red5SP $1.50

2007 ALL STARS — 153

❑ Purple Passion/Pearl Yellow/7SP $5.00
❑ **Purple Passion/Pearl Yellow/PR5 .... $3.00**

2007

2007 ALL STARS
2007 · 154

❑ Dodge Charger/M Champagne/5SP $3.00

2007 ALL STARS
2007 · 154

❑ Dodge Charger/Red/5SP $1.50

2007 ALL STARS
2007 · 155

❑ Dodge Tomahawk/Black/TMHK $1.50

2007 ALL STARS
2007 · 155

❑ Dodge Tomahawk/Yellow/TMHK $1.50

2007 ALL STARS
2007 · 156

❑ Dodge Sidewinder/M Dark Teal/5SP $1.50

2007 ALL STARS
2007 · 156

❑ Dodge Sidewinder/M Lt. Blue/5SP $1.50

MYSTERY
2007 · 157

❑ 1970 Plymouth Barracuda/Black/
   PR5 black windows $1.50

* Mystery cars are priced as loose, out of package, vehicles.

MYSTERY
2007 · 157

❑ 1970 Plymouth Barracuda/Black/
   PR5 clear windows $5.00

* Mystery cars are priced as loose, out of package, vehicles.

MYSTERY 2007 157

❏ 1970 Plymouth Barracuda/M Dark Red/PR5 $1.50

* Mystery cars are priced as loose, out of package, vehicles.

MYSTERY 2007 158

❏ What-4-2/Black/Blue10SP $5.00
❏ **What-4-2/Black/BluePR5** **$1.50**

* Mystery cars are priced as loose, out of package, vehicles.

MYSTERY 2007 158

❏ What-4-2/Pearl White/OH5SP $1.50

* Mystery cars are priced as loose, out of package, vehicles.

MYSTERY 2007 159

❏ Corvette C6/M Red/PR5 .... $1.50

* Mystery cars are priced as loose, out of package, vehicles.

MYSTERY 2007 159

❏ Corvette C6/Yellow/PR5 .... $1.50

* Mystery cars are priced as loose, out of package, vehicles.

MYSTERY 2007 160

❏ Symbolic/Neon Lt. Green/5SP................... $1.50

* Mystery cars are priced as loose, out of package, vehicles.

MYSTERY 2007 161

❏ Power Rage/Chrome/BlueOH5SP.............. $1.50

* Mystery cars are priced as loose, out of package, vehicles.

MYSTERY 2007 161

❏ Power Rage/Gold Chrome/RedCM6 .... $8.00
❏ **Power Rage/Gold Chrome/RedOH5SP** .. **$1.50**

* Mystery cars are priced as loose, out of package, vehicles.

MYSTERY 2007 162

❏ Batmobile (Animated)/Black/
  PR5 black motor $1.50
❏ Batmobile (Animated)/Black/
  PR5 chrome motor $3.00

* Mystery cars are priced as loose, out of package, vehicles.

MYSTERY 2007 163

❏ Side Draft/Grey/PR5 .... $1.50

* Mystery cars are priced as loose, out of package, vehicles.

MYSTERY 2007 164

❏ Sand Stinger/M Dark Orange/
  OR5SP front, 5SP rear $1.50

* Mystery cars are priced as loose, out of package, vehicles.

MYSTERY 2007 165

❏ 1965 Pontiac Bonneville/Flat Black/10SP .. $3.00

* Mystery cars are priced as loose, out of package, vehicles.

MYSTERY 2007 165

❏ 1965 Pontiac Bonneville/Red/10SP............ $3.00

* Mystery cars are priced as loose, out of package, vehicles.

MYSTERY 2007 166

❏ Maserati MC12/M Dark Blue/10SP $1.50

* Mystery cars are priced as loose, out of package, vehicles.

MYSTERY 2007 167

❏ Volkswagon Beetle/M Green/10SP $3.00

* Mystery cars are priced as loose, out of package, vehicles.

MYSTERY 2007 167

❏ Volkswagon Beetle/M Magenta/10SP $3.00

* Mystery cars are priced as loose, out of package, vehicles.

MYSTERY 2007 168

❑ Dodge M80/M Silver/RedPR5 .... $1.50

* Mystery cars are priced as loose, out of package, vehicles.

MYSTERY 2007 169

❑ F-Racer/White/GoldPR5 .... $1.50

* Mystery cars are priced as loose, out of package, vehicles.

MYSTERY 2007 170

❑ Bugatti Veyron/M Yellow/Gold10SP............ $1.50

* Mystery cars are priced as loose, out of package, vehicles.

MYSTERY 2007 170

❑ Bugatti Veyron/Pearl White/10SP $1.50

* Mystery cars are priced as loose, out of package, vehicles.

MYSTERY 2007 171

❑ Battle Spec/Chrome/OH5SP $1.50

* Mystery cars are priced as loose, out of package, vehicles.

MYSTERY 2007 172

❑ Corvette Stingray/M Orange/5SP $1.50

* Mystery cars are priced as loose, out of package, vehicles.

MYSTERY 2007 173

❑ Steel Flame/Flat Black/OH5SP $1.50

* Mystery cars are priced as loose, out of package, vehicles.

MYSTERY 2007 174

❑ Riley & Scott Mk III/M Lt. Blue/10SP.......... $5.00
❑ **Riley & Scott Mk III/M Lt. Blue/WSP........ $1.50**

* Mystery cars are priced as loose, out of package, vehicles.

MYSTERY

 2007 175

❏ Track T/Flat Grey/5SP black interior $1.50
❏ **Track T/Flat Grey/5SP tan interior $5.00**

* Mystery cars are priced as loose, out of package, vehicles.

MYSTERY

2007 175

❏ **Track T/White/3SP $5.00**
❏ Track T/White/SB....................................... $1.50

* Mystery cars are priced as loose, out of package, vehicles.

MYSTERY

2007 176

❏ Rapid Transit/Orange/WhitePR5 .... $1.50

* Mystery cars are priced as loose, out of package, vehicles.

MYSTERY

2007 176

❏ Rapid Transit/Red/WhitePR5...................... $1.50

* Mystery cars are priced as loose, out of package, vehicles.

MYSTERY

2007 177

❏ Road Rocket/Gold Chrome/GoldY5 .... $1.50

* Mystery cars are priced as loose, out of package, vehicles.

MYSTERY

2007 178

❏ Fish'd & Chip'd/M Brown/10SP $1.50

* Mystery cars are priced as loose, out of package, vehicles.

MYSTERY

2007 179

❏ Chaparral 2D/Blue/PR5 .... $1.50

* Mystery cars are priced as loose, out of package, vehicles.

MYSTERY

2007 180

❏ Super Comp Dragster/Black/Gold5SP $1.50

* Mystery cars are are priced as loose, out of package, vehicles.

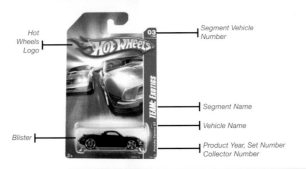

Hot Wheels Logo

Segment Vehicle Number

Segment Name

Vehicle Name

Blister

Product Year, Set Number Collector Number

2008 NEW MODELS 1 OF 40
2008 **001**

❏ '07 Shelby GT-500/Black/Y5 .... $1.50

2008 NEW MODELS 1 OF 40
2008 **001**

❏ '07 Shelby GT-500/Blue/BlackOH5SP $1.50

2008 NEW MODELS 1 OF 40
2008 **001**

❏ '07 Shelby GT-500/Pearl White/Y5 .... $3.00

2008 NEW MODELS 1 OF 40
2008 **001**

❏ '07 Shelby GT-500/Red/Y5 .... $3.00

2008 NEW MODELS 2 OF 40
2008 **002**

❏ Spector/Satin Silver Green/GreenOH5SP.. $1.50

2008 NEW MODELS 2 OF 40
2008 **002**

❏ Spector/Satin Silver Red/RedOH5SP $1.50

2008 New Models 2 of 40

❏ Spector/Silver Blue/BlueOH5SP $1.50

2008 New Models 3 of 40

❏ Audi R8/Black/OH5SP $1.50

2008 New Models 3 of 40

❏ Audi R8/M Black/10SP $1.50

2008 New Models 4 of 40

❏ Rat Bomb/Red/Black SK5 front BlackOH5SP back $1.50
❏ Rat Bomb/Purple/SK5 front OH5SP back .. $1.50

2008 New Models 4 of 40

❏ Rat Bomb/Satin Purple/SK5 front, OH5SP rear $3.00

2008 New Models 4 of 40

❏ Rat Bomb/Unpainted Grey Base/SK5 front OH5SP back $10.00
❏ Rat Bomb/Unpainted Unpainted Base/SK5 front OH5SP back $4.00

2008 New Models 5 of 40

❏ '69 Dodge Coronet Super Bee/M Grey/5SP $2.00

2008 New Models 5 of 40

❏ '69 Dodge Coronet Super Bee/Pearl White/5SP $2.00

❑ '69 Dodge Coronet Super Bee/Pearl Yellow/5SP $2.00
❑ **'69 Dodge Coronet Super Bee/Pearl Yellow/5SP w/o side stripe** **$5.00**

❑ '69 Dodge Coronet Super Bee/Red black base/5SP $2.00
❑ **'69 Dodge Coronet Super Bee/Red chrome base/5SP** **$2.00**

❑ Dragtor/M Dark Red/OH5SP front SK5 back $1.50

❑ Dragtor/M Green/SK5 front, OH5SP rear .. $1.50

❑ Dragtor/Pearl White/OH5SP front SK5 back $1.50

❑ Custom '77 Dodge Van/Grey/RedOH5SP $2.00

❑ Custom '77 Dodge Van/M Brown/GoldOH5SP $1.50

❑ **Custom '77 Dodge Van/Magenta tint windows/5SP $4.00**
❑ Custom '77 Dodge Van/Magenta blue windows/5SP $10.00

2008

2008 New Models 7 of 40

❑ Custom '77 Dodge Van/Pearl Yellow/RedOH5SP $1.50

2008 New Models 8 of 40

❑ Corvette Grand Sport/Black/PR5................ $3.00

2008 New Models 8 of 40

❑ Corvette Grand Sport/Dark Blue/PR5 silver vents $3.00
❑ **Corvette Grand Sport/Dark Blue/PR5 .... $3.00**

2008 New Models 8 of 40

❑ Corvette Grand Sport/M Grey/PR5 .... $3.00

2008 New Models 8 of 40

❑ Corvette Grand Sport/Red/PR5................. $4.00
❑ **Corvette Grand Sport/Red/Y5............... $25.00**

2008 New Models 9 of 40

❑ '09 Corvette ZR1/Grey/OH5SP $2.00

2008 New Models 9 of 40

❑ '09 Corvette ZR1/M Lt.Blue/PR5 .... $2.00

2008 New Models 9 of 40

❑ '09 Corvette ZR1/Pearl Dark Yellow/PR5 .. $4.00

❑ '09 Corvette ZR1/Red/PR5 .... $2.00

❑ Canyon Carver/M Blue/MC3 .... $3.00

❑ Canyon Carver/M Gold/Gold MC3 .... $1.50

❑ Canyon Carver/M Orange/MC3 .... $1.50

❑ **Acura NSX/Black/Red10SP** $1.50
❑ Acura NSX/Black/White10SP $6.00

❑ **Acura NSX/Pearl White/White10SP** $1.50
❑ Acura NSX/Pearl Yellow chrome interior/10SP $2.00

❑ Acura NSX/Pearl Yellow grey interior/10SP $1.50

❑ Prototype H-24/Dark Green/Grey5SP $1.50

2008

❑ Prototype H-24/Lt.Blue/Orange5SP................$1.50

❑ Prototype H-24/M Grey/Grey5SP $1.50

❑ Custom '62 Chevy/Black/BlackOH5SP $1.50

❑ Custom '62 Chevy/Dark Blue/GoldOH5SP..$1.50

❑ **Custom '62 Chevy/M Dark Magenta/GoldOH5SP ... $1.50**
❑ Custom '62 Chevy/M Dark Magenta/GoldOH5SP w/o
surfboard $25.00

❑ **Custom '62 Chevy/M Dark Red/OH5SP .. $1.50**
❑ Custom '62 Chevy/M Purple/GoldOH5SP .. $3.00

❑ Fast Fish/M Green/RedOH5SP $1.50

❑ Fast Fish/M Red-Orange/RedOH5SP $1.50

2008

❏ Hummer H2 SUT/Dark Blue/OR5SP $1.50

❏ Hummer H2 SUT/M Gold/OR5SP $1.50

❏ Hummer H2 SUT/Orange/OR5SP $1.50

❏ Dodge Challenger SRT8/Green/OH5SP $2.00

❏ Dodge Challenger SRT8/M Grey/OH5SP .. $2.00

❏ Dodge Challenger SRT8/M Orange/OH5SP $2.00

❏ Dodge Challenger SRT8/Pearl White/OH5SP $2.00

❏ '69 Chevelle/M Black/5SP $1.50
❏ '69 Chevelle/M Black/5SP/5DOT $1.50

2008

2008 New Models 17 of 40

 017

❏ '69 Chevelle/M Red/5SP $1.50

2008 New Models 17 of 40

 017

❏ '69 Chevelle/M Silver/5SP $1.50

2008 New Models 17 of 40

 017

❏ '69 Chevelle/M Yellow-Gold/5SP $1.50

2008 New Models 18 of 40

 018

❏ Croc Rod/M Green/OH5SP $1.50

2008 New Models 19 of 40

 019

❏ '69 Ford Torino Talladega/Dark Blue/5SP....$1.50

2008 New Models 19 of 40

 019

❏ '69 Ford Torino Talladega/Red/5SP $1.50

2008 New Models 20 of 40

 020

❏ Bad Mudder 2/Black/OR5SP $1.50

2008 New Models 20 of 40

 020

❏ **Bad Mudder 2/Khaki-Grey black fenders/OR5SP .. $1.50**
❏ Bad Mudder 2/Khaki-Grey chrome fenders/OR5SP
$1.50

2008

☐ Bad Mudder 2/M Silver/OR5SP................. $1.50

☐ Custom Ford Bronco/M Brown/OR5SP...... $1.50

☐ Custom Ford Bronco/Pearl Yellow/OR5SP..$1.50

☐ **Custom Ford Bronco/White silver base/OR5SP ... $1.50**
☐ Custom Ford Bronco/White chrome base/OR5SP
$1.50

☐ RocketFire/Grey Black/OH5SP $1.50

☐ **RocketFire/White Flat Black/ClearOrangeOH5SP $1.50**
☐ RocketFire/White Gloss Black/ClearOrangeOH5S $8.00

☐ 2008 Lancer Evolution/Dark Blue/OH5SP ..$1.50

☐ 2008 Lancer Evolution/M Grey/Y5 .... $1.50

2008

2008 NEW MODELS 23 OF 40 — 023

❑ 2008 Lancer Evolution/M Red/10SP $1.50

2008 NEW MODELS 24 OF 40 — 024

❑ Duel Fueler/Dark Blue/Blue OH5SP $1.50

2008 NEW MODELS 25 OF 40 — 025

❑ Pass'n Gasser/Black/GY5SP/SK5 .... $1.50
❑ Pass'n Gasser/Black/LgGY5SP/SK5.......... $1.50

2008 NEW MODELS 25 OF 40 — 025

❑ Pass'n Gasser/Green/GY5SP/SK5 .... $1.50

2008 NEW MODELS 25 OF 40 — 025

❑ Pass'n Gasser/M Purple/GY5SP/SK5 .... $1.50

2008 NEW MODELS 25 OF 40 — 025

❑ Pass'n Gasser/Pearl Yellow/GY5SP/SK5 .. $1.50

2008 NEW MODELS 26 OF 40 — 026

❑ 2008 Tesla Roadster/M Lt.Blue/10SP $1.50

2008 NEW MODELS 26 OF 40 — 026

❑ 2008 Tesla Roadster/M Red/10SP $1.50

2008

❏ 2008 Tesla Roadster/M Silver/10SP $1.50

❏ Ford Mustang Fastback/Black/BlackOH5SP $3.00

❏ Ford Mustang Fastback/M Silver/BlackOH5SP $3.00

❏ Ford Mustang Fastback/Pearl White/BlackOH5SP .. $3.00

❏ Ford Mustang Fastback/Red/BlackOH5SP $3.00

❏ Impavido 1/Yellow/BlackOH5SP $1.50

❏ '70 Pontiac GTO/M Dark Red black base/5SP $1.50
❏ '70 Pontiac GTO/M Dark Red chrome base/5SP $1.50

❏ '70 Pontiac GTO/M Lt.Blue/5SP $1.50

2008 New Models 29 of 40 — 029
❑ '70 Pontiac GTO/M Orange/5SP $1.50

2008 New Models 30 of 40 — 030
❑ Amazoom/M Lt.Green/10SP $1.50

2008 New Models 30 of 40 — 030
❑ Amazoom/M Red-Orange/Yellow10SP $1.50

2008 New Models 31 of 40 — 031
❑ '08 Ford Focus/Blue/10SP $1.50

2008 New Models 31 of 40 — 031
❑ '08 Ford Focus/Pearl Yellow/10SP $1.50

2008 New Models 31 of 40 — 031
❑ '08 Ford Focus/Red/10SP $1.50

2008 New Models 32 of 40 — 032
❑ Urban Agent/Satin Black Green/BlackOH5SP $1.50

2008 New Models 32 of 40 — 032
❑ Urban Agent/Satin Grey Red/BlackOH5SP $1.50

2008

❏ Ferrari FXX/Black/PR5 .... $2.00

❏ Ferrari FXX/Pearl Yellow/PR5 .... $2.00

❏ Ferrari FXX/Red/PR5 .... $2.00

❏ **Madfast/Dark Blue silver logo/OH5SP/SK5 .... $1.50**
❏ Madfast/Dark Blue black logo/OH5SP/SK5 .... $1.50

❏ H2GO/M Orange/MW $1.50

❏ Carbonator/Clear Green/OH5SP $1.50

❏ Camaro Convertible Concept/M Blue/OH5SP $2.00

❏ Camaro Convertible Concept/M Red-Orange/OH5SP $2.00

2008 New Models 37 of 40

☐ Camaro Convertible Concept/Pearl White/OH5SP $2.00

2008 New Models 38 of 40

☐ Ferrari GTO/Pearl Yellow/5SP $2.00

2008 New Models 38 of 40

☐ Ferrari GTO/Red/5SP $2.00

2008 New Models 38 of 40

☐ Ferrari GTO/Satin Copper/5SP $2.00

2008 New Models 39 of 40

☐ '65 Volkswagen Fastback/M Blue/5SP $20.00

2008 New Models 40 of 40

☐ Twin Mill III/Pearl Orange/BlackOH5SP $1.50

2008 All-Stars 1 of 36

☐ CUL8R/Blue/OH5SP $1.50

2008 All-Stars 1 of 36

☐ CUL8R/Flat Black/GoldOH5SP $1.50

2008

❏ CUL8R/M Gold/OH5SP $1.50

❏ La Troca/Dark Olive Green/5SP $3.00

❏ La Troca/Flat Brown/5SP............................ $1.50

❏ **La Troca/M Gold/GoldWSP $1.50**
❏ La Troca/M Gold/5SP $1.50

❏ La Troca/M Purple/WSP $1.50

❏ Sand Stinger/Dark Green/5SP front, OR5SP rear $1.50

❏ Sand Stinger/M Burgundy/OR5SP/5SP $1.50

❏ Sand Stinger/M Lt.Gold/OR5SP/5SP $1.50

2008

2008 All-Stars 4 of 36 — 2007 044

❑ Arachnorod/Green/5SP143731 .... $1.50

2008 All-Stars 4 of 36 — 2008 044

❑ Arachnorod/M Blue/5SP $1.50

2008 All-Stars 4 of 36 — 2008 044

❑ Arachnorod/Pearl Orange/5SP $1.50

2008 All-Stars 5 of 36 — 2008 045

❑ '63 Split Window/M Gold/5SP $1.50

2008 All-Stars 5 of 36 — 2008 045

❑ '63 Split Window/M Purple/5SP $1.50

2008 All-Stars 6 of 36 — 2008 046

❑ **Night Burner/Aqua Blue/YellowOH5SP .. $1.50**
❑ Night Burner/Aqua Blue/Yellow5SP $4.00

2008 All-Stars 6 of 36 — 2008 046

❑ Night Burner/M Magenta/RedOH5SP $1.50

2008 All-Stars 7 of 36 — 2008 047

❑ **Honda Civic Si/Flat Black/10SP $2.00**
❑ Honda Civic Si/Flat Black/OH5SP $2.00

2008

❏ Honda Civic Si/Gold/GoldOH5SP $1.50

❏ Honda Civic Si/M Silver/OH5SP (K-Mart) .. $3.00

❏ Fire-Eater/Red/5SP $1.50

❏ Fire-Eater/Yellow/5SP $1.50

❏ '32 Ford Delivery/Champagne/RL5SP $1.50

❏ **'32 Ford Delivery/M Blue/5SP.................. $1.50**
❏ '32 Ford Delivery/M Blue/RL5SP................. $1.50

❏ Aston Martin V8 Vantage/Black/PR5 .... $1.50

❏ Aston Martin V8 Vantage/M Dark Blue/PR5 .... $1.50

2008

2008 All-Stars 10 of 36 050

❑ Aston Martin V8 Vantage/M Silver/PR5...... $1.50

2008 All-Stars 10 of 36 050

❑ Aston Martin V8 Vantage/Pearl White/PR5 .... $1.50

2008 All-Stars 11 of 36 051

❑ Swoop Coupe/Dark BurgundySK5 front, 5DOT rear $1.50

2008 All-Stars 11 of 36 051

❑ **Swoop Coupe/Grey burgundy base/5DOT/SK5 ...** $1.50
❑ Swoop Coupe/Grey chrome base/5DOT/SK5 $1.50

2008 All-Stars 11 of 36 051

❑ **Swoop Coupe/Pearl White black base/5DOT/SK5** $1.50
❑ Swoop Coupe/Pearl White chrome base/5DOT/SK5
$1.50

2008 All-Stars 12 of 36 052

❑ HW450F/Dark Blue/ORMC $1.50

2008 All-Stars 12 of 36 052

❑ HW450F/M Red/ORMC.............................. $1.50

2008 All-Stars 13 of 36 053

❑ Screamin' Hauler/M Orange/5SP $1.50

2008

053

❑ Screamin' Hauler/Yellow/5SP $1.50

  054

❑ Mad Propz/Black White/Micro5SP.............. $1.50

  054

❑ Mad Propz/Olive Green/Micro5SP $1.50

  055

❑ **Semi Fast II/Pearl Purple/Lg5SP** **$1.50**
❑ Semi Fast II/Pearl Purple/10SP................. $1.50

  055

❑ **Semi Fast II/Red/5SP**............................... **$1.50**
❑ Semi Fast II/Red/Lg5SP $1.50

  056

❑ Hyper Mite/M Blue/PR5/5SP $1.50

  056

❑ Hyper Mite/Orange/YellowPR5/5SP $1.50

  056

❑ Hyper Mite/Pearl Purple/Red5SP $1.50

2008

2008 ALL-STARS 17 OF 36 — 2008 057
❑ Roll Cage/Black/OR5SP $1.50

2008 ALL-STARS 17 OF 36 — 2008 057
❑ Roll Cage/Dark Green/OR5SP $1.50

2008 ALL-STARS 17 OF 36 — 2008 057
❑ Roll Cage/Grey/OR5SP $1.50

2008 ALL-STARS 18 OF 36 — 2008 058
❑ 65 Chevy Impala/Blue/BlackOH5 .... $1.50

2008 ALL-STARS 18 OF 36 — 2008 058
❑ 65 Chevy Impala/Flat Black/WhiteOH5 ...... $1.50

2008 ALL-STARS 18 OF 36 — 2008 058
❑ 65 Chevy Impala/M Silver/WSP (K-Mart) .. $3.00

2008 ALL-STARS 18 OF 36 — 2008 058
❑ 65 Chevy Impala/Magenta/OrangeWSP $1.50

2008 ALL-STARS 19 OF 36 — 2008 059
❑ Split Decision/Dark Blue/OH5SP $1.50

2008

❑ Split Decision/Red/10SP $1.50

❑ Plymouth GTX/M Blue/BlackOH5SP (K-Mart) $3.00

❑ Plymouth GTX/M Green/BlackOH5SP $2.00

❑ Plymouth GTX/Orange/BlackOH5SP $2.00

❑ '41 Willys/Dark Blue/Gold5SP $1.50

❑ '41 Willys/M Gold/Gold5SP $1.50

❑ '41 Willys/M Red/Gold5SP $1.50

❑ Go Kart/M Lt.Green/5DOT......................... $1.50

❑ Go Kart/M Red-Orange/5DOT $1.50

❑ Covelight/M Dark Grey/OH5SP $1.50

❑ Covelight/Pearl White/BlackOH5SP $1.50

❑ Buzz Bombs/Yellow/GoldOH5SP $1.50

❑ '07 Cadillac Escalade/M Cranberry/OH5SP $1.50

❑ '07 Cadillac Escalade/M Grey/OH5SP $1.50

❑ '07 Cadillac Escalade/Pearl White/OH5SP $1.50

❑ Tooned Enzo Ferrari/Flat Black/GoldPR5 .. $1.50

❑ Tooned Enzo Ferrari/Red/PR5 .... $1.50

❑ Track T/Black/5DOT $1.50

❑ Track T/Dark Blue/5DOT $1.50

❑ Track T/M Copper/5DOT $1.50

❑ Ferrari 360 Modena/Black/PR5 .... $1.50

❑ Ferrari 360 Modena/Pearl Yellow/PR5 ...... $1.50

❑ '40 Ford/Black/5SP $1.50

❑ '40 Ford/Dark Blue/5SP $1.50

2008 All-Stars 29 of 36
2008 069

❏ '40 Ford/M Copper/5SP $1.50

2008 All-Stars 29 of 36
2008 069

❏ '40 Ford/Purple/5SP $1.50

2008 All-Stars 30 of 36
2008 070

❏ 1965 Pontiac GTO/Champagne/5SP (K-Mart) $4.00

2008 All-Stars 30 of 36
2008 070

❏ 1965 Pontiac GTO/M Magenta/5SP $2.00

2008 All-Stars 30 of 36
2008 070

❏ 1965 Pontiac GTO/M Teal/5SP $2.00

2008 All-Stars 30 of 36
2008 070

❏ 1965 Pontiac GTO/Orange/5SP $2.00

2008 All-Stars 31 of 36
2008 071

❏ Toyota Baja Truck/Dark Blue/OR5SP $1.50

2008 All-Stars 31 of 36
2008 071

❏ Toyota Baja Truck/M Green/OR5SP $1.50

2008

❏ Saleen S7/Dark Blue/PR5 .... $2.00

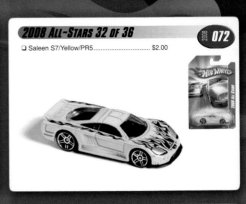

❏ Saleen S7/Yellow/PR5................................ $2.00

❏ Sling Shot/Black/PR5 .... $1.50

❏ Sling Shot/Pearl White/OH5SP $1.50

❏ Super Tuned/M Blue/PR5 .... $1.50

❏ Super Tuned/Pearl White/PR5 .... $1.50

❏ Sweet 16 II/M Blue/White5SP $1.50

❏ Sweet 16 II/M Copper/Red5SP $1.50

2008

2008 All-Stars 35 of 36 — 075
❑ Sweet 16 II/Pearl White/5SP $1.50

2008 All-Stars 36 of 36 — 076
❑ '62 Chevy/Black/PR5 (K-Mart).................... $1.50

2008 All-Stars 36 of 36 — 076
❑ '62 Chevy/M Green/PR5 .... **$1.50**
❑ '62 Chevy/M Green/5SP $1.50

2008 All-Stars 36 of 36 — 076
❑ '62 Chevy/Pearl White/PR5 .... $1.50

Web Trading Cars 1 of 24 — 077
❑ Chevy Camaro Concept/Pearl Orange/PR5 .... $2.00

Web Trading Cars 1 of 24 — 077
❑ Chevy Camaro Concept/Red/PR5.............. $2.00

Web Trading Cars 2 of 24 — 078
❑ MX48 Turbo/Blue/3SP $1.50

Web Trading Cars 2 of 24 — 078
❑ MX48 Turbo/M Red/3SP $1.50

2008

❏ So Fine/Black/WSP $1.50

❏ **So Fine/M Purple/WSP** **$1.50**
❏ So Fine/Red/5SP $3.00

❏ Meyers Manx/Lt.Green/5SP $3.00

❏ Meyers Manx/M Magenta/5SP $3.00

❏ Nissan Skyline/Black/PR5 .... $1.50

❏ Nissan Skyline/M Gold/PR5 .... $1.50

❏ Whip Creamer II/Green/5SP $1.50

❏ Whip Creamer II/Red/5SP $1.50

2008

❑ Austin-Healey/Dark Green/5SP $1.50

❑ Austin-Healey/M Grey/5SP $1.50

❑ Mega-Duty/M Blue/5DOT $1.50

❑ Mega-Duty/M Copper/5DOT $2.00
❑ Mega-Duty/M Copper/OR5SP $3.00

2008

❑ Cadillac Sixteen/M Lt.Blue/PR5................. $1.50

❑ Cadillac Sixteen/Pearl Grey/LtBluePR5 .... $1.50

❑ Pony-Up/Blue/OH5SP $1.50

❑ Pony-Up/M Green/OH5SP $1.50

❑ Dodge Concept Car/Black/GoldPR5 .... $1.50

❑ Dodge Concept Car/Pearl White/PR5 .... $1.50

❑ Pikes Peak Celica/Lt. Green/WSP $1.50

❑ Pikes Peak Celica/Red/WSP $1.50

❑ At-A-Tude/Burgundy/PR5 .... $1.50

❑ At-A-Tude/M Blue/PR5 .... $1.50

❑ 1/4 Mile Coupe/Yellow/5SP $1.50

❑ 1/4 Mile Coupe/Flat Black & Red/5SP $1.50

2008

WEB TRADING CARS 15 OF 24 — 091 2008

❑ '70 Chevelle SS/Black/5SP $2.00

WEB TRADING CARS 15 OF 24 — 091 2008

❑ '70 Chevelle SS/Grey/5SP $2.00

WEB TRADING CARS 16 OF 24 — 092 2008

❑ Greased Lightnin'/Dark Blue/PR5 .... $1.50

WEB TRADING CARS 16 OF 24 — 092 2008

❑ Greased Lightnin'/Pearl White/PR5 .... $1.50

WEB TRADING CARS 17 OF 24 — 093 2008

❑ '70 Dodge Challenger Hemi/M Orange/PR5 .... $3.00

WEB TRADING CARS 17 OF 24 — 093 2008

❑ '70 Dodge Challenger Hemi/M Red/PR5.... $3.00

WEB TRADING CARS 18 OF 24 — 094 2008

❑ Maelstrom/M Orange/PR5 .... $1.50

WEB TRADING CARS 18 OF 24 — 094 2008

❑ Maelstrom/M Purple/PR5 .... $1.50

2008

❑ **Ford GT-40/M Blue/Orange5SP** **$1.50**
❑ Ford GT-40/M Blue/ChromeOrange5SP $1.50

❑ Ford GT-40/Pearl White/ChromeBlue5SP.. $1.50

❑ Splittin' Image/Lt.Olive Green/5SP $1.50

❑ **Splittin' Image/Pearl White chrome base/5SP $1.50**
❑ Splittin' Image/Pearl White unpainted base/5SP $1.50

❑ '69 Camaro/Black/PR5 .... $3.00

❑ '69 Camaro/Pearl Yellow/PR5 .... $3.00

❑ AMG-Mercedes CLK DTM/M Blue/PR5 .... $1.50

❑ AMG-Mercedes CLK DTM/M Copper/PR5 .... $1.50

2008

WEB TRADING CARS 23 OF 24
2008 **099**

❑ What-4-2/Clear Blue/PR5 .... $1.50

WEB TRADING CARS 23 OF 24
2008 **099**

❑ What-4-2/Clear Purple/PR5 .... $1.50

WEB TRADING CARS 24 OF 24
2008 **100**

❑ Brutalistic/Neon Green/YellowPR5 .... $1.50

WEB TRADING CARS 24 OF 24
2008 **100**

❑ Brutalistic/Pearl Grey/YellowPR5 .... $1.50

TRACK STARS 1 OF 12
2008 **101**

❑ Nitro Doorslammer/Lt. Green/BlackOH5SP black base $1.50
❑ **Nitro Doorslammer/Lt. Green/BlackOH5SP grey
base** **$3.00**

TRACK STARS 2 OF 12
2008 **102**

❑ RD-02/Dark Green/GreenOH5SP $1.50

TRACK STARS 3 OF 12
2008 **103**

❑ **Sup Dogg/Pearl White/GoldPR5.............. $1.50**
❑ Sup Dogg/Pearl White/GoldOH5SP $1.50

TRACK STARS 4 OF 12
2008 **104**

❑ Rogue Hog/Silver/WhitePR5 .... $1.50

2008

❑ Motoblade/Pearl Yellow Chrome/Yellow5SP $1.50
❑ Motoblade/M Red/OH5SP $1.50

❑ CCM Country Club Muscle/Red/PR5 ...... $1.50
❑ CCM Country Club Muscle/Red/5DOT $1.50

❑ Vulture/Blue/PR5 .... $1.50
❑ Vulture/Blue/OH5SP $1.50

❑ Battle Spec/Orange/PR5 .... $1.50
❑ Battle Spec/Orange/OH5SP $1.50

❑ Chrysler Firepower Concept/Flat Black/Red10SP $1.50

❑ Lancer Evolution VII/Red/Y5 .... $1.50

❑ Accelium/M Grey/BlueTint/Y5 .... $1.50

❑ Trak-Tune/Clear Yellow/Gold10SP $1.50

2008

Hot Wheels

Team: Exotics 1 of 4
❑ Lotus Esprit/Pearl Dark Yellow/PR5 .... $1.50

Team: Exotics 2 of 4
❑ Enzo Ferrari/Dark Blue/PR5 .... $2.00

Team: Exotics 3 of 4
❑ Porsche Carrera GT/Black/PR5 .... $1.50

Team: Exotics 4 of 4
❑ Zotic/Pearl White/BlackPR5 .... $1.50

Team: Surf's Up 1 of 4
❑ Hummer H3T Concept/Dark Blue/OR5SP $1.50

Team: Surf's Up 2 of 4
❑ '40s Woodie/M Red-Orange/5SP $1.50

Team: Surf's Up 3 of 4
❑ Switchback/Pearl White/PR5..................... $1.50

Team: Surf's Up 4 of 4
❑ Surf Crate/M Lt.Blue/5SP $1.50

2008

❏ Jet Threat 4.0/M Black/Gold10SP $1.50

❏ Shadow Jet/Dark Blue/Red5SP................. $1.50

❏ Firestorm/M Grey/RedOH5SP $1.50

❏ Jet Threat 3.0/Olive Green/Red10SP $1.50

❏ T-Bucket/Olive Green/Grey5SP $1.50

❏ Dieselboy/Brown/BlackOH5SP $1.50

❏ Rat-ified/Flat Black/Black5SP $1.50

❏ Way 2 Fast/Flat Grey/Grey5SP $1.50

HOT WHEELS

TEAM: VOLKSWAGEN 1 OF 4 — 2008 129

❑ Volkswagen Beetle/Black/5SP $2.00

TEAM: VOLKSWAGEN 2 OF 4 — 2008 130

❑ Volkswagen New Beetle Cup/Orange/White10SP $2.00

TEAM: VOLKSWAGEN 3 OF 4 — 2008 131

❑ Baja Beetle/M Dark Red/5SP $4.00

TEAM: VOLKSWAGEN 4 OF 4 — 2008 132

❑ **Volkswagen Golf GTI/M Lt.Blue/Y5 .... $2.00**
❑ Volkswagen Golf GTI/Pearl White/PR5 ...... $2.00

TEAM: MUSCLE MANIA 1 OF 4 — 2008 133

❑ Pontiac GTO Judge/Grey/5SP $2.00

TEAM: MUSCLE MANIA 2 OF 4 — 2008 134

❑ '68 Plymouth Hemi 'Cuda/M Red/5SP $3.00

TEAM: MUSCLE MANIA 3 OF 4 — 2008 135

❑ '69 Dodge Charger/Green/5SP $2.00

TEAM: MUSCLE MANIA 4 OF 4 — 2008 136

❑ Chevy Nova/Red/BlackOH5SP $2.00

2008

❑ Boom Box/Pearl Dark Yellow/RedPR5 ...... $1.50

❑ Dodge Ram 1500/Pearl Yellow/OR5SP $2.00
❑ **Dodge Ram 1500/Pearl Yellow/5SP $1.50**

❑ Nissan Titan/M Burgundy/Black/RedOH5SP $1.50

❑ Custom '69 Chevy/M Dark Blue/PR5 .... $1.50

❑ **Ford GTX1/Flat Black/GoldOH5SP.......... $2.00**
❑ Ford GTX1/Flat Black/Gold5SP................. $2.00

❑ Ford F-150/M Dark Blue/OR5SP............... $1.50

❑ Mustang Cobra/M Dark Orange/WSP $3.00

❑ Deuce Roadster/Grey/5SP $1.50

2008

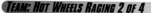

TEAM: HOT WHEELS RACING 1 OF 4
❑ Chaparral 2D/M Dark Blue/OH5SP $1.50
❑ **Chaparral 2D/M Dark Blue/PR5 .... $1.50**

2008 **145**

TEAM: HOT WHEELS RACING 2 OF 4

❑ Dodge Charger Stock Car/M Dark Blue/OH5SP $1.50

2008 **146**

TEAM: HOT WHEELS RACING 3 OF 4

❑ Double Vision/M Dark Blue/PR5 .... $1.50

2008 **147**

TEAM: HOT WHEELS RACING 4 OF 4

❑ **Nissan Silvia/M Dark Blue/Y5 .... $1.50**
❑ Nissan Silvia/M Dark Blue/OH5SP $1.50

2008 **148**

TEAM: CUSTOM BIKES 1 OF 4

❑ Pit Cruiser/M Red/MC3 .... $1.50

2008 **149**

TEAM: CUSTOM BIKES 2 OF 4

❑ Airy 8/Purple/MC5 .... $1.50

2008 **150**

TEAM: CUSTOM BIKES 3 OF 4

❑ Scorchin' Scooter/Blue/WhiteMC3.............. $1.50

2008 **151**

TEAM: CUSTOM BIKES 4 OF 4

❑ Hammer Sled/Teal/MC3 .... $1.50

2008 **152**

2008

Beckett Price Guide to: **131**

2008 153

❑ Buick Grand National/Gold/OH5SP $1.50

2008 154

❑ **Shelby Cobra 427 S/C Dark Green/3SP.. $3.00**
❑ Shelby Cobra 427 S/C Dark Green/small3SP front, 3SP rear $25.00

2008 155

❑ '57 Chevy/Pearl White/Red5SP.................. $1.50

2008 156

❑ Sooo Fast/Purple/5SP $1.50

2008 157

❑ Mustang Funny Car/Black/5SP $4.00

2008 158

❑ Jaded/Flat Olive Green/5SP $1.50

2008 159

❑ Dragster/Grey/5SP $1.50

2008 160

❑ Fiat 500c/Red/Gold5SP $1.50

2008

TREASURE HUNTS 1 OF 12
❑ Chrysler 300C HEMI/Flat Black M Green/OH5SP $15.00

2008 **161**

TREA$URE HUNT$ 1 OF 12
❑ Chrysler 300C HEMI/Flat Black Spectraflame Green/RR5SP $30.00

2008 **161**

TREASURE HUNTS 2 OF 12
❑ '70 Plymouth Road Runner/Olive Green/5SP $30.00

2008 **162**

TREA$URE HUNT$ 2 OF 12
❑ '70 Plymouth Road Runner/Spectraflame Olive Green/RR $80.00

2008 **162**

TREASURE HUNTS 3 OF 12
❑ Rockster/M Green/OR5SP $10.00

2008 **163**

TREA$URE HUNT$ 3 OF 12
❑ Rockster/Spectraflame Green/ORCT $20.00

2008 **163**

TREASURE HUNTS 4 OF 12
❑ 2005 Ford Mustang GT/M Gold/GoldChromeOH5SP $10.00

2008 **164**

TREA$URE HUNT$ 4 OF 12
❑ 2005 Ford Mustang GT/Spectraflame Gold/GoldRR5SP $30.00

2008 **164**

2008

❏ Hot Bird/M Gold/5SP $15.00

❏ Hot Bird/Spectraflame Copper/5SP $30.00

❏ Qombee/M Gold Flat Black/PR5 .... $10.00

❏ Qombee/Spectraflame Copper/RRP $20.00

❏ Dodge Challenger Funny Car/M Dark Brown/5SP $10.00

❏ Dodge Challenger Funny Car/Spectraflame
Brown/GYRR $25.00

❏ '06 Dodge Viper/Orange/OH5SP.............. $10.00

❏ '06 Dodge Viper/Spectraflame Orange/OH5SP $30.00

TREASURE HUNTS 9 OF 12

❑ 16 Angels/Dark Blue/RL5SP $10.00

TREA$URE HUNT$ 9 OF 12

❑ 16 Angels/Spectraflame Dark Blue/RLRR5SP $20.00

TREASURE HUNTS 10 OF 12

❑ '64 Buick Riviera/Magenta/WSP $10.00

TREA$URE HUNT$ 10 OF 12

❑ '64 Buick Riviera/Spectraflame Magenta/SSO5SP $25.00

TREASURE HUNTS 11 OF 12

❑ Drift King/Black/OH5SP $10.00

TREA$URE HUNT$ 11 OF 12

❑ Drift King/Spectraflame Black/SSO5SP .. $20.00

TREASURE HUNTS 12 OF 12

❑ '69 Chevy Camaro/M Blue-Grey/OH5SP $20.00

TREA$URE HUNT$ 12 OF 12

❑ '69 Chevy Camaro/Spectraflame
Steel Blue/SSO5SP $40.00

❏ '69 Corvette/Black/GoldOH5SP..................$1.50

❏ Bon Voyage/M Blue/Black&Red OH5SP $1.50

❏ '66 Chevy Nova/M Burgandy/PR5..............$2.00

❏ Cloak and Dagger/Clear Blue/PR5 ....$1.50

❏ Jester/Clear/Black&WhiteOH5SP $1.50

❏ Altered State/Red/5SP................................$1.50

❏ Ballistik/Red/Y5 ....$1.50

❏ **Mustang Mach 1/Pearl Yellow dark blue logos/5SP $3.00**
❏ Mustang Mach 1/Pearl Yellow lt.blue logos/5SP $3.00

2008

MYSTERY 9 OF 24

❏ Ford Shelby GR-1 Concept/Dark Green/BlackOH5SP $1.50

MYSTERY 10 OF 24

❏ Hooligan/Flat Black/RL5SP $1.50

MYSTERY 11 OF 24

❏ Shoe Box/M Red/Red5SP $1.50

MYSTERY 12 OF 24

❏ Monoposto/Blue/PR5................................ $1.50

MYSTERY 13 OF 24

❏ Lancia Stratos/Silver/White5SP.................. $1.50

MYSTERY 14 OF 24

❏ Super Tsunami/M Dark Orange/OrangePR5 ...... $1.50

MYSTERY 15 OF 24

❏ Lane Splitter/Pearl White/RedOH5SP $1.50

MYSTERY 16 OF 24

❏ GT-03/Grey/PR5 .... $2.00

❏ Callaway C-7/Pearl Grey/OrangeOH5SP .. $1.50

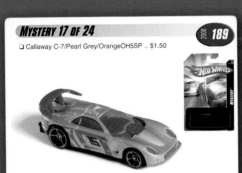

❏ Scion XB/Clear Blue/PR5 .... $1.50

❏ Corvette C6-R/M Dark Blue/OH5SP $2.00

❏ Saltflat Racer/Blue/MagentaPR5 .... $1.50

❏ Ford Mustang GT Concept/Black/Y5.......... $3.00

❏ '57 T-Bird/Orange/5SP.............................. $1.50

❏ '58 Corvette/M Blue/5SP $2.00

❏ Technetium/M Teal/OH5SP $1.50

2008

Hot Wheels Logo

Segment Vehicle Number

Vehicle Name

Blister

Segment Name

Mainline Vehicle Number

2009

2009 NEW MODELS 1 OF 42

❑ 2009 Nissan GT-R/Pearl White/DkChr10SP........ $1.50
❑ 2009 Nissan GT-R/Pearl White/10SP $1.50

2009 NEW MODELS 1 OF 42

❑ 2009 Nissan GT-R/M Red/10SP......................... $1.50

2009 NEW MODELS 1 OF 42

❑ 2009 Nissan GT-R/M Silver/10SP $1.50

2009 NEW MODELS 2 OF 42

❑ Circle Tracker/Orange/RedBlackOH5SP $2.00

2009 NEW MODELS 2 OF 42

❑ Circle Tracker/Red/GoldBlackOH5SP.................. $1.50

2009 NEW MODELS 3 OF 42

❑ Corvette C6/M Blue/PR5 .... $2.00

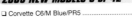

2009 NEW MODELS 3 OF 42

❑ Corvette C6/M Orange/PR5................................. $2.00

2009 NEW MODELS 4 OF 42

❑ Brit Speed/M Blue/OH5SP.................................. $1.50

2009 NEW MODELS 4 of 42

- ❑ Brit Speed/M Green chrome base/OH5SP $1.50
- ❑ Brit Speed/M Green grey base/OH5SP $1.50

2009 NEW MODELS 5 of 42

- ❑ Ferrari 250 GTO/Black/WSP $2.00

2009 NEW MODELS 5 of 42

- ❑ Ferrari 250 GTO/Red/WSP $2.00
- ❑ Ferrari 250 GTO/Red black side vent/WSP $4.00

2009 NEW MODELS 5 of 42

- ❑ Ferrari 250 GTO/Yellow/WSP $3.00

2009 NEW MODELS 6 of 42

- ❑ 5 Alarm/Orange/OrangeBlackPR $1.50

2009 NEW MODELS 6 of 42

- ❑ 5 Alarm/Red/RedBlackPR $1.50

2009 NEW MODELS 7 of 42

- ❑ '70 Buick GSX/Pearl Yellow/5SP $8.00

2009 NEW MODELS 7 of 42

- ❑ '70 Buick GSX/Red/5SP $4.00

2009

❏ '70 Buick GSX/White/5SP.................................... $2.00

❏ '69 Mercury Cougar Eliminator/Dark Blue/5SP.... $1.50

❏ '69 Mercury Cougar Eliminator/M Purple/5SP..... $1.50

❏ '69 Mercury Cougar Eliminator/M Purple/RL5SP $1.50

❏ '69 Mercury Cougar Eliminator/M Dark Orange/5SP $1.50

❏ OCC Splitback/Black/OrangeMC3...................... $2.00

❏ OCC Splitback/M Blue/MC3 .... $2.00

❏ OCC Splitback/M Red/MC3 .... $2.00
❏ OCC Splitback/M Red/MC5 front MC3 rear....... $20.00

2009 NEW MODELS 10 OF 42
❏ Bye Focal II/M Blue/OH5SP $1.50

2009 NEW MODELS 10 OF 42
❏ Bye Focal II/M Magenta/OH5SP $1.50

2009 NEW MODELS 11 OF 42
❏ 2009 Ford F-150/M Black/RedBlackOH5SP.........$1.50

2009 NEW MODELS 11 OF 42
❏ 2009 Ford F-150/M Blue/Red/BlackOH5SP $1.50

2009 NEW MODELS 11 OF 42
❏ 2009 Ford F-150/M Grey/RedBlackOH5SP..........$1.50

2009 NEW MODELS 12 OF 42
❏ Mid Mill/Black/OH5SP/SK5 .... $1.50

2009 NEW MODELS 12 OF 42
❏ Mid Mill/Satin Blue/Orange/BlackOH5SP/SK5 .... $1.50

2009 NEW MODELS 13 OF 42
❏ '71 Dodge Demon/Green/5SP $3.00

2009

❏ '71 Dodge Demon/M Purple/5SP.........................$3.00

❏ '71 Dodge Demon/Pearl Yellow/5SP $2.00

❏ Fast Gassin/Pearl White/5SP $1.50

❏ Fast Gassin/Red/5SP $1.50

❏ Fast Gassin/Satin Green/5SP..............................$1.50

❏ Custom '53 Cadillac/M Gold/WSP $2.00

❏ Custom '53 Cadillac/M Lt. Blue/WSP $2.00

❏ Custom '53 Cadillac/M Purple/5SP......................$2.00

2009

2009 NEW MODELS 16 of 42

❏ AMC Javelin AMX/M Black/5SP (K-Mart) $5.00

2009 NEW MODELS 16 of 42

❏ AMC Javelin AMX/M Green/5SP $2.00

2009 NEW MODELS 16 of 42

❏ AMC Javelin AMX/Pearl Orange/5SP $2.00

2009 NEW MODELS 17 of 42

❏ Volkswagen Type 181/Flat Beige/OH5SP $1.50

2009 NEW MODELS 17 of 42

❏ Volkswagen Type 181/M Blue/OH5SP $1.50
❏ Volkswagen Type 181/M Blue/5SP $1.50

2009 NEW MODELS 17 of 42

❏ Volkswagen Type 181/M Orange/OH5SP............. $1.50

2009 NEW MODELS 18 of 42

❏ Avant Garde/M Gold/OH5SP $1.50

2009 NEW MODELS 18 of 42

❏ Avant Garde/M Lt.Blue/OH5SP $1.50

2009

❑ '70 Chevelle SS Wagon/M Blue/5SP $1.50

❑ '70 Chevelle SS Wagon/M Gold/5SP $2.00

❑ '70 Chevelle SS Wagon/M Gold/RL5SP $2.00

❑ '70 Chevelle SS Wagon/Yellow/5SP $1.50

❑ Dune It Up/Pearl Yellow/OR5SP/5SP $1.50

❑ Dune It Up/Orange/OR5SP/5SP $1.50

❑ Lamborghini Reventon/M Grey/PR5 .... $6.00

❑ Tri & Stop Me/Black/Gold/BlackOH5SP $1.50

2009 NEW MODELS 22 of 42

☐ Tri & Stop Me/M Orange/Orange/BlackOH5SP... $1.50

2009 NEW MODELS 23 of 42

☐ Custom V-8 Vega/M Red/5SP $1.50

2009 NEW MODELS 23 of 42

☐ Custom V-8 Vega/M Teal/5SP $1.50

2009 NEW MODELS 23 of 42

☐ Custom V-8 Vega/Pearl Yellow/5SP $1.50

2009 NEW MODELS 24 of 42

☐ La Fasta/Pearl Yellow/YellowBlackOH5SP $1.50

2009 NEW MODELS 24 of 42

☐ La Fasta/Red/Red/BlackOH5SP $1.50

2009 NEW MODELS 25 of 42

☐ Custom '41 Willys Coupe/M Blue/5SP $2.00

2009 NEW MODELS 25 of 42

☐ Custom '41 Willys Coupe/M Orange/5SP $2.00

❑ '10 Camaro SS/M Orange/OH5SP $2.00

❑ '10 Camaro SS/M Silver/OH5SP $2.00

❑ Custom '42 Jeep CJ-2A/Khaki/OR5SP/5SP $1.50

❑ Custom '42 Jeep CJ-2A/Olive Green/OR5SP/5SP $1.50

❑ Barbaric/Pearl Pink/Chrome/BlackOH5SP $1.50

❑ '70 Plymouth AAR Cuda/Green/5SP $2.00

❑ '70 Plymouth AAR Cuda/M Magenta/5SP $2.00

❑ '70 Plymouth AAR Cuda/Orange/5SP $2.00

2009

2009 NEW MODELS 30 OF 42
❏ F1 Racer/M Blue/Orange/BlackOH5SP $2.00

2009 NEW MODELS 31 OF 42
❏ '66 Ford Fairlane GT/M Red/RL5SP (Walmart) ... $2.00

2009 NEW MODELS 31 OF 42
❏ '66 Ford Fairlane GT/M Red/5SP $2.00

2009 NEW MODELS 31 OF 42
❏ '66 Ford Fairlane GT/M Teal/5SP $2.00

2009 NEW MODELS 32 OF 42
❏ Tread Air/M Gold/BlackMicro5SP $1.50

2009 NEW MODELS 33 OF 42
❏ Triumph TR6/Dark Green/5SP $1.50

2009 NEW MODELS 33 OF 42
❏ Triumph TR6/M Silver/Blue5SP $1.50

2009 NEW MODELS 34 OF 42
❏ Fast FeLion/M Dark Red/OH5SP $1.50

2009

❑ Fast FeLion/M Silver/OH5SP............................... $1.50

❑ Four-1/Pearl White/Green5SP............................. $1.50

❑ Gearonimo/Red/Red/BlackPR5............................ $1.50

❑ Datsun Bluebird 510/Black/BlackOH5SP $1.50

❑ Datsun Bluebird 510/M Blue/BlackOH5SP $3.00

❑ Datsun Bluebird 510/M Copper/Chrome/BlackOH5SP $1.50

❑ Ferrari California/Red/PR5.................................... $3.00
❑ Ferrari California/Satin Copper/5SP $2.00

❑ Ford GT LM/Pearl White/PR5............................... $2.00

2009

❏ Ford GT LM/Satin Blue/PR5 .... $2.00

❏ Draggin' Tail/M Orange/5SP $2.00

❏ 2010 Ford Mustang GT/M Blue/PR5 .... $4.00

❏ 2010 Ford Mustang GT/Pearl Yellow/PR5 .... $4.00

❏ 2010 Ford Mustang GT/Red/PR5 .... $2.00

❏ Pedal de Metal/Lavender/Orange/BlackSK5 .... $1.50

2009

❏ '65 Ford Mustang/M Red/5SP $10.00

❏ '65 Ford Mustang/Spectraflame Red/RLRR $20.00

❏ '57 Plymouth Fury/M Orange/WL5SP.................. $6.00

❏ '57 Plymouth Fury/Spectraflame Copper/WLRR5SP $12.00

❏ Bad Bagger/M Blue-Purple/MC3 .... $10.00

❏ Bad Bagger/Spectraflame Blue/RRMC5............ $20.00

❏ Fire-Eater/M Red/5SP.. $10.00

❏ Fire-Eater/Spectraflame Red/RLRR $20.00

❏ '37 Ford/M Teal/5SP $10.00

❏ '37 Ford/Spectraflame Teal/Red-ChromeWWRR $20.00

2009

2009 TREASURE HUNTS 6 OF 12 — 2009 048

❏ '34 Ford/M Black/5SP $10.00

2009 TREA$URE HUNT$ 6 OF 12 — 2009 048

❏ '34 Ford/Spectraflame Black/WWRR $20.00

2009 TREASURE HUNTS 7 OF 12 — 2009 049

❏ Custom '53 Chevy/M Purple/5SP211631 .... $12.00

2009 TREA$URE HUNT$ 7 OF 12 — 2009 049

❏ Custom '53 Chevy/Spectraflame Purple/WWRR $25.00

2009 TREASURE HUNTS 8 OF 12 — 2009 050

❏ Bone Shaker/M Gold/5SP $12.00

2009 TREA$URE HUNT$ 8 OF 12 — 2009 050

❏ Bone Shaker/Spectraflame Gold/5SPBLING $25.00

2009 TREASURE HUNTS 9 OF 12 — 2009 051

❏ '49 Merc/M Copper/WW5SP $8.00

2009 TREA$URE HUNT$ 9 OF 12 — 2009 051

❏ '49 Merc/Spectraflame Copper/WWRR $15.00

2009

❑ '55 Chevy/M Magenta/5SP $15.00

❑ '55 Chevy/Spectraflame Magenta/WWRR........ $30.00

❑ GMC Motorhome/M Grey/OrangeBlackOH5SP $12.00
❑ GMC Motorhome/Satin Silver/RL5SP................ $40.00

❑ Neet Streeter/M Olive/5SP $8.00

❑ Neet Streeter/Spectraflame Green/RR5SP $15.00

❑ Rocketfire/Gold Chrome/GoldOH5SP................. $1.50

❑ Solar Reflex/Black/Red-BlackOH5SP................. $1.50

❑ Ultra Rage/Yellow/OH5SP $1.50

2009

2009 TRACK STARS 4 of 12

❑ Buzz Bomb/Blue/OH5SP $1.50

2009 TRACK STARS 5 of 12
❑ Dodge XP-07/M Green/PR5 .... $1.50

2009 TRACK STARS 6 of 12
❑ Nerve Hammer/Green/PR5................................. $2.00

2009 TRACK STARS 7 of 12
❑ Chrysler HEMI 300C/M Red/BLING $2.00

2009 TRACK STARS 8 of 12
❑ '69 Chevelle/Clear Blue/GoldOH5SP.................. $2.00

2009 TRACK STARS 9 of 12
❑ Synkro/Red/Red-BlackOH5SP $2.00

2009 TRACK STARS 10 of 12
❑ Covelight/Gold Chrome/White-BlackOH5SP $1.50

2009 TRACK STARS 11 of 12
❑ RD-10/Blue/OH5SP $1.50

2009

2009 TRACK STARS 12 OF 12 066
❏ Reverb/Chrome/Red5SP $1.50

2009 HW RACING 1 OF 10 067
❏ Chevroletor/M Dark Grey/OH5SP........................ $2.00

2009 HW RACING 2 OF 10 068
❏ Acura NSX/Dark Blue/RedBlackOH5SP $1.50

2009 HW RACING 2 OF 10 068
❏ Acura NSX/M Dark Red/Red-BlackOH5SP $1.50

2009 HW RACING 3 OF 10 069
❏ GP-2009/M Dark Green/GoldWSP $1.50

2009 HW RACING 3 OF 10 069
❏ GP-2009/Satin Blue/WSP $1.50

2009 HW RACING 4 OF 10 070
❏ Panoz GTR-1/M Dark Blue/WhiteOH5SP............. $1.50

2009 HW RACING 4 OF 10 070
❏ Panoz GTR-1/M Midnight Blue/RedY5 .... $1.50

2009 HW RACING 5 OF 10
2009 **071**

❏ Corvette C6R/Pearl Yellow/Orange-BlackOH5 (Walmart) $4.00

2009 HW RACING 5 OF 10
2009 **071**

❏ Corvette C6R/Satin Blue/Blue-BlackOH5 .... $2.00

2009 HW RACING 6 OF 10
2009 **072**

❏ Pro Stock Firebird/Pearl Purple/OH5SP $2.00

2009 HW RACING 6 OF 10
2009 **072**

❏ Pro Stock Firebird/Pearl White/Red5SP $2.00

2009 HW RACING 7 OF 10
2009 **073**

❏ Cabbin' Fever/Blue/WhitePR5 .... $1.50

2009 HW RACING 7 OF 10
2009 **073**

❏ Cabbin' Fever/M Red/WhitePR5 .... $1.50

2009 HW RACING 8 OF 10
2009 **074**

❏ Pass'n Gasser/Satin Brown/HWR5SP/SK5 .... $1.50

2009 HW RACING 9 OF 10
2009 **075**

❏ GT Racer/M Blue/Red5SP $2.00

2009

❏ Amazoom/Flourescent Yellow/10SP $1.50

❏ '69 Camaro/M Purple/OH5SP $4.00

❏ '69 Camaro/Orange/OH5SP $5.00

❏ '69 Camaro/Pearl Yellow/Gold-BlackOH5SP (Walmart) $5.00

❏ '67 Shelby GT-500/M Dark Burgundy/Red-BlackOH5SP $4.00

❏ '67 Shelby GT-500/M Dark Burgundy/RL5SP (Walmart) $5.00

❏ '67 Shelby GT-500/Pearl Purple/Chrome-BlackOH5SP
(K-Mart).. $5.00

❏ '67 Shelby GT-500/Pearl Yellow/BlackOH5SP $3.00

2009

2009 MUSCLE MANIA 3 of 10 — 2009 079

❑ '70 Plymouth Road Runner/Black/OrangeBlackOH5SP $2.00

2009 MUSCLE MANIA 3 of 10 — 2009 079

❑ '70 Plymouth Road Runner/M Blue/OH5SP $2.00

2009 MUSCLE MANIA 4 of 10 — 2009 080

❑ '71 Plymouth GTX/M Dark Grey/5SP (Walmart).. $2.00

2009 MUSCLE MANIA 4 of 10 — 2009 080

❑ '71 Plymouth GTX/M Dark Magenta/5SP $2.00

2009 MUSCLE MANIA 5 of 10 — 2009 081

❑ '69 Dodge Charger/M Dark Orange/5SP............. $2.00

2009 MUSCLE MANIA 5 of 10 — 2009 081

❑ '69 Dodge Charger/M Red/5SP $2.00

2009 MUSCLE MANIA 5 of 10 — 2009 081

❑ '69 Dodge Charger/Pearl White/5SP (K-Mart)..... $4.00

2009 MUSCLE MANIA 6 of 10 — 2009 082

❑ Oldsmobile 442/M Dark Copper/BlackPR5.......... $2.00

❏ Oldsmobile 442/Pearl Purple/OH5SP.................. $2.00

❏ Oldsmobile 442/Pearl White/Red-BlackPR5.........$2.00

❏ '69 Dodge Coronet Super Bee/Blue/5SP............. $2.00

❏ '69 Dodge Coronet Super Bee/M Orange/5SP.... $2.00

❏ '69 Chevelle/M Blue/WhitePR5 (K-Mart) $5.00

❏ '69 Chevelle/M Green/WhitePR5 .... $2.00

❏ '65 Mustang Fastback/M Orange/Chrome-BlackOH5SP
(K-Mart)... $6.00

❏ '65 Mustang Fastback/Pearl White/Chrome-BlackOH5SP
.... $4.00

2009

Hot Wheels™

2009 MUSCLE MANIA 10 OF 10 — 086

❑ '08 Dodge Challenger SRT8/M Dark Grey/Blue-BlackOH5
.... $2.00

2009 MUSCLE MANIA 10 OF 10 — 086

❑ '08 Dodge Challenger SRT8/M Green/Chrome-BlackOH5SP
.... $2.00

2009 MUSCLE MANIA 10 OF 10 — 086

❑ '08 Dodge Challenger SRT8/M Green/RL5SP (Walmart)
.... $3.00

2009 SPECIAL FEATURES 1 OF 10 — 087

❑ Dodge Ram 1500/M Dark Red/OR5SP (Walmart)
.... $3.00

2009 SPECIAL FEATURES 1 OF 10 — 087

❑ Dodge Ram 1500/M Green/OR5SP $1.50

2009 SPECIAL FEATURES 1 OF 10 — 087

❑ Dodge Ram 1500/M Orange/OR5SP $1.50

2009 SPECIAL FEATURES 2 OF 10 — 088

❑ Spector/Satin Black-Clear Purple/Purple-BlackOH5SP
.... $1.50

2009 SPECIAL FEATURES 3 OF 10 — 089

❑ Jet Threat 4.0/Flat Olive Green/Gold10SP.......... $1.50

❑ Jet Threat 4.0/M Purple/Gold10SP $1.50

❑ Split Decision/Clear Purple/Chrome-BlackOH5SP $1.50

❑ Cloak And Dagger/M Purple/Red-BlackOH5SP .. $1.50

❑ Cloak And Dagger/Pearl White/GoldBlackOH5SP $1.50

❑ Ground FX/M Blue/SK5 .... $1.50

❑ Ground FX/Red/SK5190331 .... $1.50

❑ Night Burner/Black/OrangeBlackOH5SP $1.50

❑ Night Burner/M Purple/Yellow-BlackOH5SP $1.50

2009

2009 SPECIAL FEATURES 8 of 10 2009 094

❑ Urban Agent/Pearl Magenta/Chrome-BlackOH5SP $1.50

2009 SPECIAL FEATURES 8 of 10 2009 094

❑ Urban Agent/Pearl White/White-BlackOH5SP $1.50

2009 SPECIAL FEATURES 9 of 10 2009 095

❑ Ferrari 512M/Dark Blue/PR5 .... $1.50

2009 SPECIAL FEATURES 9 of 10 2009 095

❑ Ferrari 512M/Pearl Yellow/PR5........................... $1.50

2009 SPECIAL FEATURES 9 of 10 2009 095

❑ Ferrari 512M/Red/PR5... $1.50

2009 SPECIAL FEATURES 10 of 10 2009 096

❑ XS-IVE/M Dark Blue/BlackOR5SP $1.50

2009 SPECIAL FEATURES 10 of 10 2009 096

❑ XS-IVE/M Red/OR5SP $1.50

2009 HW DESIGNS 1 of 10 2009 097

❑ Nitro Scorcher/Dark Green/5SP $1.50

2009 HW DESIGNS 2 OF 10

❏ HW40/Pearl White/GoldPR5............................... $1.50

2009 HW DESIGNS 3 OF 10

❏ **Hyper Mite/Black/Green-BlackPR5-Micro5SP** .$1.50
❏ Hyper Mite/Black/GreenPR5-Micro5SP $1.50

2009 HW DESIGNS 3 OF 10

❏ Hyper Mite/Pearl Orange/PR5-Micro5SP $1.50

2009 HW DESIGNS 4 OF 10

❏ Deora II/M Dark Blue/OH5SP $2.00

2009 HW DESIGNS 4 OF 10

❏ Deora II/M Dark Copper/Orange-BlackOH5SP $2.00

2009 HW DESIGNS 4 OF 10

❏ Deora II/M Purple/OH5SP $2.00

2009 HW DESIGNS 5 OF 10

❏ 16 Angels/Dark Olive Green/WhiteBlackPR5 ...... $1.50

2009 HW DESIGNS 6 OF 10

❏ Fast Fortress/M Blue Pearl White/5SP $1.50

HOT WHEELS™

2009 HW DESIGNS 6 OF 10 — 2009 — 102

❑ Fast Fortress/M Dark Blue-Grey/5SP $1.50

2009 HW DESIGNS 7 OF 10 — 2009 — 103

❑ Ballistik/M Grey/GoldOH5SP $1.50

2009 HW DESIGNS 8 OF 10 — 2009 — 104

❑ Pony Up/M Purple/Gold5SP $1.50

2009 HW DESIGNS 8 OF 10 — 2009 — 104

❑ Pony Up/Pearl Dark Yellow/5SP $1.50

2009 HW DESIGNS 9 OF 10 — 2009 — 105

❑ Scorchin' Scooter/M Purple/BlackMC3 .... $3.00

2009 HW DESIGNS 10 OF 10 — 2009 — 106

❑ Overbored 454/M Dark Orange/OH5SP $1.50

2009 HW DESIGNS 10 OF 10 — 2009 — 106

❑ Overbored 454/Satin Antifreeze Green/OH5SP .. $1.50

2009 CITY WORKS 1 OF 10 — 2009 — 107

❑ Killer Copter/Chrome $1.50

2009

❏ Killer Copter/Red.................................... $1.50

❏ i07 Chevy Tahoe/Pearl White/RedOH5SP $2.00

❏ i07 Chevy Tahoe/Red/Gold-BlackOH5SP.............$2.00

❏ Ford Fusion/Black/PR5 .... $2.00

❏ Ford Fusion/M Dark Blue/PR5............................. $1.50

❏ Ford Fusion/Pearl White/PR5 .... $1.50

❏ Armored Truck/Chrome/Gold-BlackOH5SP $1.50

❏ Armored Truck/Gold Chrome/RedBlackOH5SP .. $1.50
❏ Surfin' School Bus/Flat Brown/RL5SP................. $1.50

2009

2009 CITY WORKS 5 of 10 | 2009 111
❑ Surfin' School Bus/Flat Brown/5SP $1.50

2009 CITY WORKS 5 of 10 | 2009 111
❑ Surfin' School Bus/M Dark Grey/5SP196431 ...... $1.50

2009 CITY WORKS 6 of 10 | 2009 112
❑ Cockney Cab II/Black/GoldOH5SP $1.50

2009 CITY WORKS 6 of 10 | 2009 112
❑ Cockney Cab II/Green White/OH5SP196531 ...... $1.50

2009 CITY WORKS 6 of 10 | 2009 112
❑ Cockney Cab II/Pearl Gold/OH5SP $1.50

2009 CITY WORKS 7 of 10 | 2009 113
❑ Ice Cream Truck/M Blue/10SP $1.50

2009 CITY WORKS 7 of 10 | 2009 113
❑ Ice Cream Truck/M Purple/RL5SP (Walmart) $1.50

2009 CITY WORKS 7 of 10 | 2009 113
❑ Ice Cream Truck/M Purple/10SP $1.50

❏ Ice Cream Truck/M Red/10SP $1.50

❏ Hiway Hauler/Blue/PR5 .... $1.50

❏ Hiway Hauler/M Copper/PR5 .... $4.00

❏ Hiway Hauler/Yellow/PR5 .... $1.50

❏ Morris Wagon/White/5SP $1.50

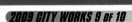

❏ Street Cleaver/Gold Chrome/5SP $1.50

❏ Chevy Silverado/Black/OH5SP $1.50

❏ '68 Chevy El Camino/M Silver/Red-BlackPR5 ..... $1.50

2009

❏ '68 Chevy El Camino/Pearl White/Gold-BlackOH5SP $1.50

❏ Baja Breaker/M Purple/OR5SP $1.50

❏ Baja Breaker/M Red/OR5SP $1.50

❏ Baja Breaker/Satin Blue/OR5SP $1.50

❏ Mad Propz/M Dark Blue/Micro5SP $2.00

❏ Custom Volkswagen Beetle/M Dark Red/Gold5SP $1.50

❏ Custom Volkswagen Beetle/M Green/5SP (K-Mart) $3.00
❏ Custom Volkswagen Beetle/M Purple/GY5SP
(Walmart) $3.00

❏ Custom Volkswagen Beetle/M Purple/White-BlackOH5SP
.... $1.50

2009

❑ Camaro Convertible Concept/M Red/OH5SP...... $3.00

❑ Jeep Scrambler/M Blue/OR5SP $1.50

❑ Jeep Scrambler/M Blue/RLOR5SP (Walmart)..... $1.50

❑ Jeep Scrambler/M Brown/BlackOR5SP $1.50

❑ Jeep Scrambler/Pearl White/OR5SP................... $1.50

❑ Morris Mini/Pearl Yellow/5SP $1.50
❑ '55 Nomad/Dark Blue/ChromeBlackOH5SP (Target)
$1.50

❑ '55 Nomad/Dark Blue/OH5SP............................. $1.50

❑ '55 Nomad/Dark Pearl Yellow/5SP $1.50

2009 HEAT FLEET 10 OF 10
❏ Midnight Otto/Flat Brown/White5SP $1.50

2009 **126**

2009 HEAT FLEET 10 OF 10

❏ **Midnight Otto/M Orange metal base/Gold3SP $1.50**
❏ Midnight Otto/M Orange plastic base/Gold3SP ... $1.50

2009 **126**

2009 FASTER THAN EVER 1 OF 10

❏ 2008 Lancer Evolution/M Dark Red/FTE............$2.00
❏ 2008 Lancer Evolution/M Dark Red/OH5SP $2.00

2009 **127**

2009 FASTER THAN EVER 1 OF 10

❏ 2008 Lancer Evolution/Pearl White/FTE.............. $2.00

2009 **127**

2009 FASTER THAN EVER 2 OF 10

❏ **Dodge Challenger Concept/M Silver/FTE** $2.00
❏ Dodge Challenger Concept/M Silver/OH5SP $2.00

2009 **128**

2009 FASTER THAN EVER 3 OF 10

❏ **Dodge Charger SRT8/Black/FTE**.......................$2.00
❏ Dodge Charger SRT8/Black/OH5SP $2.00

2009 **129**

2009 FASTER THAN EVER 4 OF 10

❏ **Duel Fueler/M Gold/FTE** $2.00
❏ Duel Fueler/M Gold/OH5SP (Target) $3.00

2009 **130**

2009 FASTER THAN EVER 4 OF 10

❏ Duel Fueler/M Green/FTE $2.00

2009 **130**

2009

2009 FASTER THAN EVER 5 OF 10

❏ Buick Grand National/M Dark Red/FTE.............. $2.00

2009 FASTER THAN EVER 5 OF 10

❏ Buick Grand National/M Grey/FTE...................... $2.00

2009 FASTER THAN EVER 6 OF 10

❏ Straight Pipes/M Dark Blue/FTE........................$2.00
❏ Straight Pipes/M Dark Blue/OH5SP $2.00

2009 FASTER THAN EVER 6 OF 10

❏ Straight Pipes/M Magenta/FTE (Walmart)........... $3.00

2009 FASTER THAN EVER 7 OF 10

❏ '66 Batmobile/Black/FTE...................................... $6.00

2009 FASTER THAN EVER 8 OF 10

❏ Lotus Concept/M Green/FTE..............................$2.00
❏ Lotus Concept/M Green/OH5SP $2.00

2009 FASTER THAN EVER 9 OF 10

❏ '09 Corvette ZR1/M Green/FTE $3.00
❏ '09 Corvette ZR1/M Green/OH5SP $3.00

2009 FASTER THAN EVER 9 OF 10

❏ '09 Corvette ZR1/Satin Copper/FTE $3.00
❏ '09 Corvette ZR1/Satin Copper/OH5SP $3.00

2009 FASTER THAN EVER 10 of 10

2009 **136**

- ❑ **Chevy Nova/Black/FTE** $2.00
- ❑ Chevy Nova/Black/OH5SP $2.00

2009 FASTER THAN EVER 10 of 10

2009 **136**

- ❑ **Chevy Nova/M Blue/FTE (K-Mart)** $4.00
- ❑ Chevy Nova/M Copper/OH5SP (Target) $3.00

2009 FASTER THAN EVER 10 of 10

2009 **136**

- ❑ Chevy Nova/M Copper/FTE...............................$2.00

2009 REBEL RIDES 1 of 10

2009 **137**

- ❑ Airy 8/M Magenta/GoldMC5................................$1.50

2009 REBEL RIDES 1 of 10

2009 **137**

- ❑ Airy 8/M Teal/GoldMC5 ....$1.50

2009 REBEL RIDES 2 of 10

2009 **138**

- ❑ '32 Ford Vicky/M Blue-Grey metal base/Red5SP $1.50

2009 REBEL RIDES 2 of 10

2009 **138**

- ❑ **'32 Ford Vicky/M Blue-Grey plastic base/Red5SP $1.50**
- ❑ '32 Ford Vicky/M Blue-Grey/Red10SP $1.50

2009 REBEL RIDES 2 of 10

2009 **138**

- ❑ '32 Ford Vicky/M Dark Copper/10SP..................$1.50

2009

❏ Custom '62 Chevy/M Dark Copper/Gold-BlackOH5SP $1.50

❏ '64 Lincoln Continental/M Gold/OH5SP............... $1.50

❏ '64 Lincoln Continental/M Magenta/OH5SP $2.00

❏ Custom Ford Bronco/M Dark Blue/GoldOR5SP .. $1.50

❏ Roll Cage/M Dark Red/OR5SP........................... $1.50

❏ Bad Mudder 2/M Grey/OR5SP $1.50

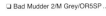

❏ Bad Mudder 2/M Red/OR5SP $1.50

❏ Mustang Mach 1/M Green/Chrome-BlackOH5SP (Walmart)
.... $4.00

2009

2009 REBEL RIDES 8 OF 10
❑ Mustang Mach 1/M Orange/RL5SP (Walmart) $4.00

2009 REBEL RIDES 8 OF 10
❑ Mustang Mach 1/M Orange/White-BlackOH5SP....$2.00

2009 REBEL RIDES 8 OF 10
❑ Mustang Mach 1/M Purple/WhiteBlackOH5SP.... $2.00

2009 REBEL RIDES 9 OF 10
❑ Dixie Challenger/M Dark Blue/5SP...................... $2.00

2009 REBEL RIDES 9 OF 10
❑ Dixie Challenger/Red/5SP $2.00

2009 REBEL RIDES 10 OF 10
❑ Ford F-150/M Grey/OR5SP $1.50

2009 DREAM GARAGE 1 OF 10
❑ 2006 Dodge Viper/M Dark Grey/OH5SP $1.50

2009 DREAM GARAGE 1 OF 10
❑ 2006 Dodge Viper/M Silver/Chrome-BlackOH5SP $1.50

2009

❏ '69 Corvette ZL-1/M Blue/PR5 .... $2.00

❏ '69 Corvette ZL-1/M Red/PR5 .... $2.00

❏ '67 Camaro/Satin Blue/Blue-BlackPR5 .... $3.00

❏ '67 Camaro/Satin Blue/RL5SP (Walmart) $5.00

❏ '67 Camaro/Satin Grey/5SP (K-Mart) $5.00

❏ '67 Camaro/Satin Pale Green/5SP $3.00

❏ Lamborghini Murcielago/M Green/PR5 .... $2.00

❏ Lamborghini MurciÉlago/M Orange/Chrome-BlackPR5 $2.00

2009

2009 DREAM GARAGE 4 OF 10 150

❑ Lamborghini Murcielago/Pearl White/BlackPR5 .. $2.00

2009 DREAM GARAGE 5 OF 10 151

❑ Hummer H2/M Copper/OR5SP $1.50

2009 DREAM GARAGE 5 OF 10 151

❑ Hummer H2/M Purple/OR5SP $1.50

2009 DREAM GARAGE 6 OF 10 152

❑ Mercedes AMG CLK DTM/M Blue/GoldPR5 .... $1.50

2009 DREAM GARAGE 7 OF 10 153

❑ Ferrari F430 Spider/Pearl White/BlackOH5SP $2.00

2009 DREAM GARAGE 7 OF 10 153

❑ Ferrari F430 Spider/Yellow/Yellow-BlackOH5SP . $2.00

2009 DREAM GARAGE 8 OF 10 154

❑ Canyon Carver/M Black/OrangeMC3 .... $2.00

2009 DREAM GARAGE 8 OF 10 154

❑ Canyon Carver/M Red/GoldMC3 .... $1.50

2009

❏ Porsche Carrera GT/M Grey/PR5........................ $2.00

❏ Porsche Carrera GT/Yellow/PR5 .... $2.00

❏ Nissan Skyline GT-R R32/M Dark Blue/BlackPR5 $1.50

❏ Nissan Skyline GT-R R32/M Dark Gold/BlackPR5 $1.50

❏ Tail Dragger/M Blue/WSP $1.50

❏ Tail Dragger/Pearl Purple/WSP $1.50

❏ Dairy Delivery/Flat Dark Olive Green/5SP215831 $1.50

❏ Dairy Delivery/M Silver/Red5SP $1.50

2009

2009 MODIFIED RIDES 2 OF 10
2009 158

☐ Dairy Delivery/Yellow/RL5SP (Walmart) $2.00

2009 MODIFIED RIDES 2 OF 10
2009 158

☐ Dairy Delivery/Yellow/5SP $1.50

2009 MODIFIED RIDES 3 OF 10
2009 159

☐ Way 2 Fast/M Magenta/GoldPR5 .... $1.50

2009 MODIFIED RIDES 4 OF 10
2009 160

☐ Sooo Fast/Pearl Yellow/5SP-SK5 .... $1.50

2009 MODIFIED RIDES 4 OF 10
2009 160

☐ Sooo Fast/Satin Black/White5SP SK5 .... $1.50

2009 MODIFIED RIDES 5 OF 10
2009 161

☐ Asphalt Assault/M Green/10SP $1.50

2009 MODIFIED RIDES 5 OF 10
2009 161

☐ Asphalt Assault/Pearl Yellow/10SP $1.50

2009 MODIFIED RIDES 6 OF 10
2009 162

☐ Honda Civic Si/M Dark Grey/OrangeBlackOH5SP $1.50

❏ Honda Civic Si/Pearl Lt. Blue/Red-BlackOH5SP..... $1.50

❏ Fiat 500/Antifreeze Green/5SP $1.50

❏ 40 Ford Pickup/M Gold/5DOT.............................$3.00
❏ 40 Ford Pickup/M Gold/5SP $2.00

❏ 40 Ford Pickup/M Purple/5SP $4.00

❏ 40 Ford Pickup/Red/5SP.....................................$1.50
❏ 40 Ford Pickup/Red/5DOT $2.00

❏ At-A-Tude/Dark Green/Gold5SP $1.50

❏ At-A-Tude/M Red/Gold5SP $1.50

❏ Deuce Roadster/M Teal/5SP $1.50

HOT WHEELS™

2009 MYSTERY CARS 1 OF 24 167
❑ Corvette Grand Sport/Pearl White/Gold-BlackPR5 $2.00

2009 MYSTERY CARS 2 OF 24 168
❑ Ferrari F430 Challenge/Red/WhiteY5.................. $2.00

2009 MYSTERY CARS 3 OF 24 169
❑ Shadow Mk IIa/Dark Green/5SP.......................... $1.50

2009 MYSTERY CARS 4 OF 24 170
❑ Ford Shelby Cobra Concept/M Red/PR5 .... $3.00

2009 MYSTERY CARS 5 OF 24 171
❑ Fast Fish/M Dark Blue/WhiteOH5SP.................. $1.50

2009 MYSTERY CARS 6 OF 24 172
❑ Shell Shock/Orange/OH5SP............................... $1.50

2009 MYSTERY CARS 7 OF 24 173
❑ Ford GTX1/M Silver/RedBlackOH5SP $1.50

2009 MYSTERY CARS 8 OF 24 174
❑ Ferrari 250/M Black/10SP................................... $2.00

2009

❑ Drift King/M Silver/RedBlackOH5SP $1.50

❑ Nitro Doorslammer/M Purple/OrangeChromeOH5SP $1.50

❑ Chevy Camaro Concept/M Blue/Yellow5SP $2.00

❑ Gangster Grin/Pearl White/Red-BlackPR5 .... $1.50

❑ Mitsubishi Double Shotz/M Blue/Orange10SP $1.50

❑ '40 Ford Convertible/M Grey/Gold5SP $1.50

❑ Dodge Concept Car/M Red/OH5SP $1.50

❑ Prototype H-24/Red/Black5SP............................ $1.50

2009

2009 MYSTERY CARS 17 OF 24   183

❑ Rogue Hog/Gold Chrome/OH5SP $1.50

2009 MYSTERY CARS 18 OF 24   184

❑ Shelby Cobra Daytona Coupe $2.00

2009 MYSTERY CARS 19 OF 24   185

❑ Split Vision/Satin Antifreeze Green/RedBlackOH5SP $1.50

2009 MYSTERY CARS 20 OF 24   186

❑ '08 Ford Focus/Satin Black/RedPR5 .... $1.50

2009 MYSTERY CARS 21 OF 24   187

❑ Rat Bomb/M Green/YellowBlackOH5SP SK5 ......$1.50

2009 MYSTERY CARS 22 OF 24   188

❑ '07 Shelby GT500/M Purple/Gold10SP $2.00

2009 MYSTERY CARS 23 OF 24   189

❑ Custom '64 Galaxie/Satin Black/Red5SP $2.00

2009 MYSTERY CARS 24 OF 24   190

❑ Quad Rod/Chrome/RedBlackOH5SP $1.50

2009

2009 BONUS SECTION

COLLECTOR EDITION MAIL-IN PROMO

2009 COLLECTOR EDITION MAIL-IN PROMO 1 OF 4

❏ '55 Chevy Panel/M Burgandy/WLRR5SP
(K-Mart)...$30.00

2009 COLLECTOR EDITION MAIL-IN PROMO 2 OF 4

❏ '67 Pontiac GTO/M Burgandy/WLRR5SP
(K-Mart)...$15.00

2009 COLLECTOR EDITION MAIL-IN PROMO 3 OF 4

❏ Volkswagen Fastback/M Burgandy/WLRRMag
(Toys R Us)...$40.00

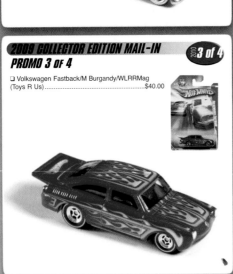

2009 COLLECTOR EDITION MAIL-IN PROMO 4 OF 4

❏ Heavy Chevy/M Burgandy/WLRR5SP
(K-Mart)...$40.00

2009

Hot Wheels Logo

Segment Vehicle Number

01 44

'67 SHELBY GT-500™

Vehicle Name

2010 NEW MODELS

Segment Name

Blister

3+   R0916   001/240

Mainline Vehicle Number

2010

❏ '67 Shelby GT500/M Blue/5SP $4.00

❏ '67 Shelby GT500/M Dark Green/5SP $4.00

❏ '67 Shelby GT500/Pearl White/5SP.................... $4.00

❏ Tooligan/Chrome/Yellow-BlackOH5SP $1.50

❏ Tooligan/Dark Chrome/BlueOH5SP.................... $1.50

❏ Tooligan/Gold Chrome/Red-BlackOH5SP $1.50

2010

2010 003

❏ '67 Pontiac Firebird 400/M Dark Blue/Black-Chrome
OH5SP $2.00

2010 003

❏ '67 Pontiac Firebird 400/M Green/Black-ChromeOH5SP
.... $2.00

2010 003

❏ '67 Pontiac Firebird 400/Red/White-BlackOH5SP
.... $2.00
❏ '67 Pontiac Firebird 400/Red/WhiteGY5SP (Walmart) $3.00

2010 004

❏ Volkswagen Beetle/M Champagne/5SP $1.50

2010 004

❏ Volkswagen Beetle/M Dark Blue/5SP $1.50

2010 004

❏ Volkswagen Beetle/M Dark Burgundy/5SP........ $1.50
❏ Volkswagen Beetle/M Dark Burgundy/GY5SP (Walmart)
.... $2.00

2010

❏ Scorcher/Dark Blue black hood/Black-ChromePR5
.... $1.50
❏ Scorcher/Dark Blue silver hood/Black-ChromePR5 $1.50

❏ Scorcher/M Dark Purple/Black-ChromePR5 ...... $1.50

❏ Scorcher/M Dark Red/Black-ChromePR5 .... $1.50

❏ Torque Twister/M Purple/Gold-BlackOH5SP $1.50

❏ Torque Twister/Pearl Orange/Black-ChromeOH5SP
.... $1.50

❏ Torque Twister/Satin Lt. Blue/Black-ChromeOH5SP
.... $1.50

2010

2010 NEW MODELS 7 OF 44 — 007

❑ Nissan GT-R/M Dark Blue/10SP $2.00

2010 NEW MODELS 7 OF 44 — 007

❑ Nissan GT-R/M Grey/10SP $2.00

2010 NEW MODELS 8 OF 44 — 008

❑ Fangula/M Gold/OH5SP-SK5 .... $1.50

2010 NEW MODELS 8 OF 44 — 008

❑ Fangula/M Purple/OH5SP-SK5 .... $1.50

2010 NEW MODELS 9 OF 44 — 009

❑ '10 Ford Shelby GT500/M Blue/PR5 .... $5.00

2010 NEW MODELS 9 OF 44 — 009

❑ '10 Ford Shelby GT500/M Grey/PR5.................. $5.00

2010

❏ '10 Ford Shelby GT500/Pearl Yellow/PR5 ....$5.00

❏ '09 Cadillac CTS-V/M Black/10SP $1.50

❏ '09 Cadillac CTS-V/M Burgundy/10SP $1.50

❏ '09 Cadillac CTS-V/M Silver/10SP..................... $1.50

❏ Snow Ride/M Dark Orange/Skis $2.00

❏ Snow Ride/M Dark Purple/Skis $2.00

2010

❑ Spider Rider/Brown/OR5SP $1.50
❑ Spider Rider/Lt. Green/OR5SP $1.50

❑ Spider Rider/Yellow/OR5SP $1.50

❑ Bread Box/Red/White5SP $1.50

❑ Bread Box/White/5SP $1.50

❑ Porsche 911 GT2/Black/PR5 .... $4.00

❑ '81 DeLorean DMC-12/Black/10SP $4.00

2010

❏ '81 DeLorean DMC-12/M Silver/10SP $5.00

❏ '81 DeLorean DMC-12/Satin Gold/Gold10SP $1.50

❏ Yur So Fast/M Green/WhiteY5 .... $1.50

❏ Yur So Fast/Pearl White/Black-ChromePR5 ...... $1.50

❏ Ducati 1098R/Pearl White/BlackMCPR5 .... $2.00

❏ Ducati 1098R/Red/BlackMCPR5 .... $2.00

❏ Rapid Response/Pearl White/5SP $1.50

❏ Rapid Response/Red/5SP $1.50

❏ Rapid Response/Yellow/5SP $1.50

❏ '09 Corvette Stingray Concept/M Grey/OH5SP .. $3.00

❏ '09 Corvette Stingray Concept/Pearl Lt. Blue/OH5SP
.... $2.00

❏ '09 Corvette Stingray Concept/Pearl Yellow/OH5SP..... $1.50

2010

❏ Formula Street/M Blue/Orange-BlackOH5SP $1.50

❏ Formula Street/Yellow/Red-BlackOH5SP $1.50

❏ Sting Rod II/M Black/OR5SP $1.50

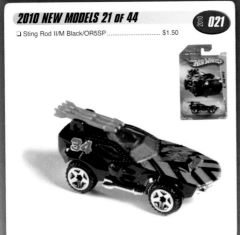

❏ Sting Rod II/Pearl Yellow/OR5SP $1.50

❏ '08 Viper SRT10 ACR/Black/Red-BlackOH5SP...... $1.50

❏ '08 Viper SRT10 ACR/Red/BlackOH5SP............ $1.50

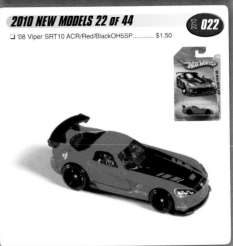

2010

2010

❏ Teegray/Black/Orange-BlackPR5........................ $1.50

❏ Teegray/Pearl White/10SP.................................. $1.50

❏ Sandblaster/Dark Olive Green/CopperOR5SP .. $1.50

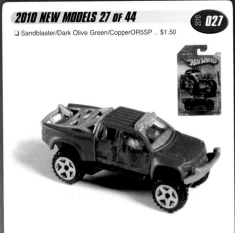

❏ **Sandblaster/Khaki/RedOR5SP $1.50**
❏ Sandblaster/Khaki/CopperOR5SP $1.50

❏ '62 Ford Mustang Concept/White/5SP $2.00

❏ '62 Ford Mustang Concept/Yellow/5SP $2.00

2010

2010 NEW MODELS 29 OF 44   2010 029
❏ Howlin' Heat/M Gold/OH5SP $2.00

2010 NEW MODELS 30 OF 44   2010 030
❏ '49 Drag Merc/M Purple/5SP $3.00

2010 NEW MODELS 31 OF 44   2010 031
❏ Salt Shaker/Chrome/RedSK5 .... $1.50

2010 NEW MODELS 31 OF 44   2010 031
❏ Salt Shaker/Pearl White/WhiteSK5 .... $1.50

2010 NEW MODELS 32 OF 44   2010 032
❏ '10 Infiniti G37/M Steel Blue/J5 .... $3.00

2010 NEW MODELS 33 OF 44   2010 033
❏ '71 Maverick Grabber/Blue/5SP $1.50

2010

❑ '71 Maverick Grabber/M Gold/5SP $1.50

❑ '71 Maverick Grabber/Pearl Dark Yellow/5SP $1.50

❑ Ferrari 458 Italia/Red/OH5SP $4.00

❑ Scoopa Di Fuego/M Red/OH5SP $1.50

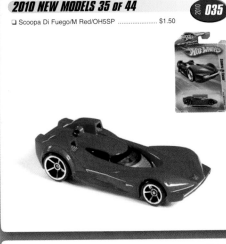

❑ Scoopa Di Fuego/M Silver/Red-BlackOH5SP $1.50

❑ '71 Dodge Charger/Lime Green/5SP $2.00

2010

2010 NEW MODELS 36 OF 44

❏ '71 Dodge Charger/Orange/5SP $2.00

2010 NEW MODELS 36 OF 44

❏ '71 Dodge Charger/Yellow/5SP $3.00

2010 NEW MODELS 37 OF 44

❏ Nissan 370Z/M Blue/PR5 .... $1.50

2010 NEW MODELS 37 OF 44

❏ Nissan 370Z/Pearl Yellow/PR5 .... $1.50

2010 NEW MODELS 38 OF 44

❏ Custom '10 Camaro SS/M Green/Yellow-BlackPR5.... $6.00

2010 NEW MODELS 38 OF 44

❏ Custom '10 Camaro SS/M Orange/Black-ChromePR5
.... $4.00

2010

❏ Tyrrell P34 Six Wheeler/Blue/Black5SP $1.50

❏ '86 Monte Carlo SS/Black/5SP $4.00

❏ Toyota Land Cruiser FJ40/Pearl Yellow/OR5SP
.... $1.50
❏ Toyota Land Cruiser FJ40/Blue/OR5SP $2.00

❏ Batmobile/Black/10SP $5.00

❏ Dodge Charger Drift Car/M Black/Blue-BlackOH5SP
.... $1.50

❏ Dodge Charger Drift Car/M Dark Blue/Black-ChromeOH5SP
.... $1.50

2010 NEW MODELS 43 of 44

043

❏ Dodge Charger Drift Car/M Silver/Black-ChromeOH5SP
.... $1.50

2010 NEW MODELS 44 of 44

044

❏ '67 Chevelle SS 396/M Aqua/5SP $2.00

2010 NEW MODELS 44 of 44

044

❏ '67 Chevelle SS 396/M Champagne/5SP $3.00
❏ '67 Chevelle SS 396/M Champagne/BFG5SP (Walmart)
.... $4.00

2010 NEW MODELS 44 of 44

044

❏ '67 Chevelle SS 396/M Dark Red/5SP $3.00

2010 TREASURE HUNTS 1 of 12

045

❏ Custom '53 Cadillac/Pearl Pink/5SP $15.00

2010 TREA$URE HUNT$ 1 of 12

045

❏ Custom '53 Cadillac/Spectraflame Pink/WWRR..... $20.00

❑ Chevroletor/White-Satin Red/Red-ChromeOH5SP.....$12.00

❑ Chevroletor/Spectraflame White-Red/RLPC5........ $20.00

❑ Rat Bomb/M Silver/Red-BlackOH5SP $4.00

❑ Rat Bomb/Spectraflame Silver/BlackRLOH5SP......$12.00

❑ Shelby Cobra Daytona Coupe/Orange/OH5SP.......$8.00

❑ Shelby Cobra Daytona Coupe/Spectraflame Orange/OH5SP
.... $15.00

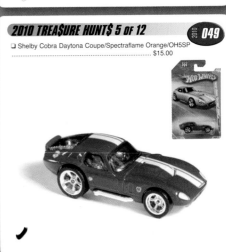

2010

2010 TREASURE HUNTS 6 of 12 2010 050

❑ Gangster Grin/M Purple/10SP $10.00

2010 TREA$URE HUNTS 6 of 12 2010 050

❑ Gangster Grin/Spectraflame Violet/DISH $20.00

2010 TREASURE HUNTS 7 of 12 2010 051

❑ Ford GTX1/M Dark Blue/OH5SP $10.00
❑ Ford GTX1/Spectraflame Blue/5SPBLING $30.00

2010 TREASURE HUNTS 8 of 12 2010 052

❑ Old Number 5.5/Red/White-Red5SP $12.00

2010 TREA$URE HUNT$ 8 of 12 2010 052

❑ Old Number 5.5/Spectraflame Red/White-RedOH5SP
.... $25.00

2010 TREASURE HUNTS 9 of 12 2010 040

❑ '69 Ford Torino Talladega/M Dark Olive Green/BlackGY5SP
.... $8.00

2010

❏ '69 Ford Torino Talladega/Spectraflame Dark Green/Black
GY5SP $20.00

❏ Chevy Camaro Concept/Orange/PR5 .... $12.00

❏ Chevy Camaro Concept/Spectraflame Copper/RREx
.... $30.00

❏ Baja Beetle/Matte Black-Pearl Yellow/OR5SP........ $15.00

❏ Baja Beetle/Matte Black-Spectraflame Yellow/ORRR
.... $40.00

❏ Twin Mill III/M Green/OH5SP............................. $1.50

2010

2010 TRACK STARS 2 OF 12

❏ Acura NSX/M Gold/White-BlackPR5 .... $1.50

2010 TRACK STARS 4 OF 12

❏ Impavido 1/Red/GoldPR5 .... $1.50

2010 TRACK STARS 5 OF 12

❏ Mitsubishi Double Shotz/M Green/White10SP............. $1.50

2010 TRACK STARS 6 OF 12

❏ Side Draft/Satin Antifreeze/PR5.......................... $1.50

2010 TRACK STARS 7 OF 12

❏ Power Pistons/Chrome/Gold5SP........................ $1.50

2010 TRACK STARS 8 OF 12

❏ Hollowback/Pearl White/Gold-BlackOH5SP $1.50

2010

❏ Drift King/Dark Olive Green/GoldOH5SP $1.50

❏ Split Vision/Pearl White/GoldPR5 ....$2.00

❏ Motoblade/M Dark Blue/White-BlackOH5SP $2.00

❏ Dieselboy/Satin Blue/Red-BlackOH5SP $2.00

❏ 2010 Ford Mustang GT/Black/Yellow-BlackPR5......$4.00

❏ 2010 Ford Mustang GT/Blue/WhitePR5 ....$4.00

2010

2010 HW GARAGE 2 OF 10

❑ **Chevy Silverado/M Purple/Black-ChromeOH5SP**
.... **$3.00**
❑ Chevy Silverado/M Purple/BFG5SP (Walmart) .. $4.00

2010 HW GARAGE 2 OF 10

❑ Chevy Silverado/Satin Copper/Black-ChromeOH5SP
.... $3.00

2010 HW GARAGE 3 OF 10

❑ Lamborghini Reventon/M Green/PR5 .... $5.00

2010 HW GARAGE 4 OF 10

❑ Dune It Up/M Green/OR5SP-5S $1.50

2010 HW GARAGE 5 OF 10

❑ 40's Woodie/M Teal/5SP $1.50

2010 HW GARAGE 5 OF 10

❑ 40's Woodie/Pearl Yellow/5SP (Walmart $2.00

074

❏ '10 Camaro SS/Blue/OH5SP (Walmart) $6.00

074

❏ '10 Camaro SS/M Grey/OH5SP $4.00

074

❏ '10 Camaro SS/M Red/White-BlackOH5SP $4.00

075

❏ Go Kart/Blue/5SP.. $2.00

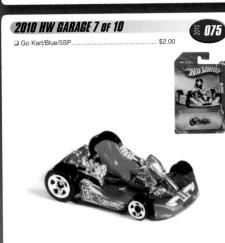

076

❏ Ferrari P4/M Dark Blue/Gold5SP........................ $2.00

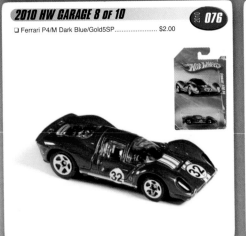

077

❏ H2GO/Black/MW $1.50

2010

2010 HW GARAGE 10 OF 10 — 2010 · 078

❏ La Fasta/M Silver/Blue-BlackOH5SP $1.50

2010 MUSCLE MANIA 1 OF 10 — 2010 · 079

❏ AMC Javelin AMX/M Blue/MC5 .... $3.00

2010 MUSCLE MANIA 1 OF 10 — 2010 · 079

❏ AMC Javelin AMX/Red/MC5 .... $2.00

2010 MUSCLE MANIA 2 OF 10 — 2010 · 080

❏ '70 Plymouth AAR Cuda/M Blue/MC5 .... $2.00

2010 MUSCLE MANIA 2 OF 10 — 2010 · 080

❏ '70 Plymouth AAR Cuda/Pearl White/MC5 ....$2.00

2010 MUSCLE MANIA 3 OF 10 — 2010 · 081

❏ '69 Cougar Eliminator/M Grey/MC5 .... $2.00

2010

❏ '69 Cougar Eliminator/M Olive Green/MC5 ....$3.00

❏ '66 Ford Fairlane GT/M Blue/MC5 (Walmart) $3.00

❏ '66 Ford Fairlane GT/M Red/MC5 .... $2.00

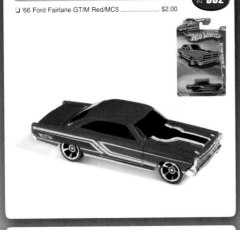

❏ '66 Ford Fairlane GT/Pearl Yellow/MC5 ....$2.00

❏ '70 Buick GSX/M Blue/MC5.............................. $1.50

❏ '70 Buick GSX/M Olive Green/MC5 (Walmart $3.00

2010

2010 MUSCLE MANIA 6 OF 10

2010 084

❏ '69 Pontiac GTO Judge/Orange/MC5 .... $2.00

2010 MUSCLE MANIA 6 OF 10

2010 084

❏ '69 Pontiac GTO Judge/Pearl Yellow/MC5 ....$2.00

2010 MUSCLE MANIA 7 OF 10

2010 085

❏ '67 Dodge Charger/M Champagne/MC5 ....$3.00

2010 MUSCLE MANIA 7 OF 10

2010 085

❏ '67 Dodge Charger/M Lt. Blue/MC5.................... $3.00

2010 MUSCLE MANIA 7 OF 10

2010 085

❏ '67 Dodge Charger/M Magenta/OH5SP $4.00
❏ '67 Dodge Charger/M Magenta/MC5 .... $4.00

2010 MUSCLE MANIA 8 OF 10

2010 086

❏ '67 Camaro/Black/MC5 .... $10.00

2010

❑ '67 Camaro/Orange/MC5 .... $6.00

❑ '70 Plymouth Superbird/Pearl White/MC5 (K-Mart)
.... $4.00

❑ '70 Plymouth Superbird/Pearl Yellow/MC5 .... $3.00

❑ '70 Plymouth Superbird/Satin Green/MC5 ....$3.00

❑ '69 Pontiac Firebird TA/Black/MC5 .... $1.50

❑ '69 Pontiac Firebird TA/M Dark Blue/MC5 (Walmart)
.... $2.00

2010

2010 MUSCLE MANIA 10 OF 10
2010 | 088

❑ '69 Pontiac Firebird TA/M Teal/MC5 .... $1.50

2010 NIGHTBURNERZ SERIES 1 OF 10
2010 | 089

❑ Super Gnat/M Purple/J5 .... $1.50

2010 NIGHTBURNERZ SERIES 2 OF 10
2010 | 090

❑ '70 Chevelle SS/M Red/J5 .... $2.00

2010 NIGHTBURNERZ SERIES 2 OF 10
2010 | 090

❑ '70 Chevelle SS/Yellow/J5 .... $2.00

2010 NIGHTBURNERZ SERIES 3 OF 10
2010 | 091

❑ 2008 Lancer Evolution/M Blue/J5 .... $1.50

2010 NIGHTBURNERZ SERIES 3 OF 10
2010 | 091

❑ 2008 Lancer Evolution/M Olive Green/GoldJ5..... $2.00

2010

❑ Asphalt Assault/M Orange/BlueJ5 .... $1.50

❑ 2009 Nissan GT-R/Black/J5 .... $2.00

❑ '70 Plymouth Road Runner/M Gold/J5 .... $2.00

❑ '70 Plymouth Road Runner/M Silver/J5.............. $2.00

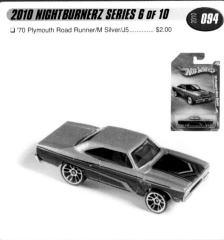

❑ '67 Custom Mustang/Red/J5 .... $2.00

❑ 24-Seven/M Red/J5 .... $2.00

2010

2010 NIGHTBURNERZ SERIES 9 OF 10 | 2010 | 097

❑ Datsun Bluebird 510/Pearl White/BlueJ5 ....$2.00

2010 NIGHTBURNERZ SERIES 10 OF 10 | 2010 | 098

❑ Volkswagen Golf GTI/M Green/J5 .... $1.50

2010 HW PERFORMANCE 1 OF 10 | 2010 | 099

❑ Ground FX/Pearl Dark Yellow/SK5 .... $1.50

2010 HW PERFORMANCE 2 OF 10 | 2010 | 100

❑ Dodge Challenger SRT8/M Black/Orange-BlackOH5SP
.... $2.00

2010 HW PERFORMANCE 2 OF 10 | 2010 | 100

❑ Dodge Challenger SRT8/M Dark Blue/Orange-BlackOH5SP
(Walmart) $3.00

2010 HW PERFORMANCE 2 OF 10 | 2010 | 100

❑ Dodge Challenger SRT8/Pearl White/Black-ChromeOH5SP
.... $2.00

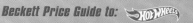

2010

❑ Camaro Convertible Concept/Dark Green/OH5SP
.... $2.00

❑ Pro Stock Firebird/Blue/5SP $1.50

❑ Pro Stock Firebird/Red/5SP............................... $1.50

❑ '57 Chevy Bel Air/Black-Silver/Red5SP $4.00

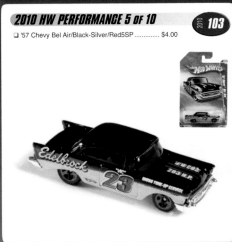

❑ '57 Chevy Bel Air/M Champagne/5SP $2.00

❑ '57 Chevy Bel Air/Red/5SP (K-Mart) $5.00

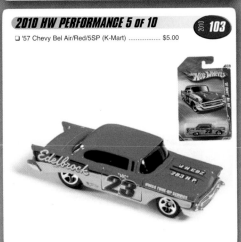

2010 HW PERFORMANCE 6 OF 10

❏ Pass' n Gasser/Dark M Green/5SP-SK5 .... $1.50

2010 HW PERFORMANCE 6 OF 10

❏ **Pass' n Gasser/Dark M Red/5SP-SK5 .... $1.50**
❏ Pass' n Gasser/Dark M Red/GY5SP (Walmart) ... $2.00

2010 HW PERFORMANCE 7 OF 10

❏ '92 Ford Mustang/M Dark Blue/5SP (K-Mart) $3.00

2010 HW PERFORMANCE 7 OF 10

❏ '92 Ford Mustang/M Dark Red/5SP $2.00

2010 HW PERFORMANCE 8 OF 10

❏ '41 Willys/Pearl Grey/BFG5SP (Walmart) $3.00
❏ '41 Willys/Pearl Grey/5SP (Walmart) $3.00

2010 HW PERFORMANCE 8 OF 10

❏ '41 Willys/ Pearl Yellow/5SP $1.50
❏ '41 Willys/Pearl Yellow/GYSP (Walmart) $3.00

2010

❑ '56 Ford F-100/M Purple/5SP (Walmart) $2.50

❑ '56 Ford F-100/M Steel Blue/5SP **$1.50**
❑ '56 Ford F-100/M Steel Blue/BFG5SP (Walmart) $2.50

❑ '56 Ford F-100/Red/5SP $3.00

❑ Dodge Ram 1500/Blue/OR5SP $1.50

❑ Dodge Ram 1500/Dark M Red/OR5SP................ **$1.50**
❑ Dodge Ram 1500/Pearl White/GoldOR5SP $1.50

❑ '07 Cadillac Escalade/Pearl Yellow/Yellow-BlackPR5
.... $1.50

2010

2010 HW CITY WORKS SERIES 2 OF 10 — 110

❏ Dodge Charger SRT8/M Black/Black-ChromeOH5SP
.... $2.00

2010 HW CITY WORKS SERIES 3 OF 10 — 111

❏ Custom '66 GTO Wagon/M Red/5SP $2.00

2010 HW CITY WORKS SERIES 4 OF 10 — 112

❏ Scorchin' Scooter/Pearl White/RedMC3 ....$1.50

2010 HW CITY WORKS SERIES 5 OF 10 — 113

❏ Hummer H2/Pearl White/OR5SP (Toys R Us) $2.00

2010 HW CITY WORKS SERIES 5 OF 10 — 113

❏ Hummer H2/Pearl Yellow/OR5SP $1.50

2010 HW CITY WORKS SERIES 6 OF 10 — 114

❏ '09 Ford F-150/M Aqua Blue/Yellow-BlackPR5....$1.50

2010

❑ '09 Ford F-150/Red/Yellow-BlackPR5 .... $1.50

❑ Rescue Ranger/M Green/Blue5SP $1.50

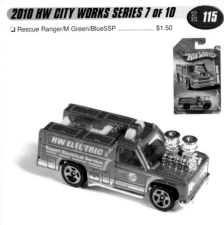

❑ Rescue Ranger/Pearl Dark Yellow/Blue5SP........$1.50

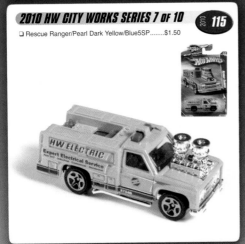

❑ GMC Motorhome/M Blue/BFG5SP (Walmart) 5.00

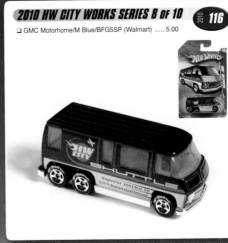

❑ GMC Motorhome/M Blue/5SP $3.00

❑ Custom '77 Dodge Van/Pearl White/OrangeOH5SP
.... $3.00

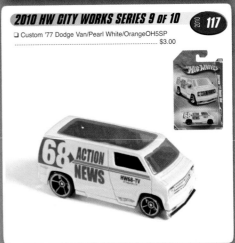

2010

❏ Four-1/Black/Blue5SP $1.50

❏ Mazda Furai/M Dark Grey/OH5SP $1.50

❏ Mazda Furai/M Red/OH5SP $1.50

❏ Scirocco GT 24/Blue/10SP $1.50

❏ Scirocco GT 24/M Red/10SP............................. $1.50

❏ Gallardo LP 560-4/Matte White/WSP $4.00

2010 ALL STARS 3 of 10

❑ Gallardo LP 560-4/Satin Black/WSP $3.00

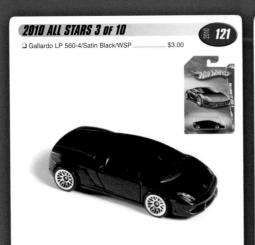

2010 ALL STARS 5 of 10

❑ Ford Focus RS/M Green/10SP $3.00

2010 ALL STARS 6 of 10

❑ '10 Aston Martin DBS/M Grey/10SP $3.00

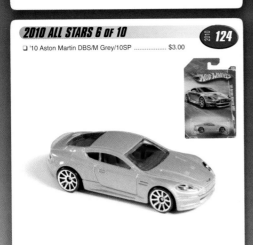

2010 ALL STARS 7 of 10

❑ '73 Ford Falcon XB/M Blue/5SP $8.00

2010 ALL STARS 7 of 10

❑ '73 Ford Falcon XB/Yellow/5SP $4.00

2010 ALL STARS 8 of 10

❑ Volkswagen SP2/Orange/5SP $2.00

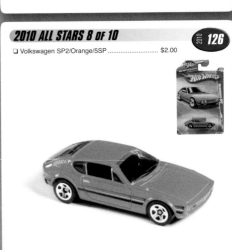

2010 ALL STARS 9 OF 10

❏ Ferrari 430 Scuderia/Red/Red-BlackPR5 (Walmart)
.... $3.00
❏ **Ferrari 430 Scuderia/Yellow/Yellow-BlackPR5 .. $4.00**

2010 ALL STARS 10 OF 10

❏ Ferrari 308 GTS/M Dark Blue/5SP $3.00

2010 FASTER THAN EVER 1 OF 10

❏ Custom V-8 Vega/Black/FTE (Walmart) $3.00

2010 FASTER THAN EVER 1 OF 10

❏ **Custom V-8 Vega/M Dark Blue/FTE $2.00**
❏ Custom V-8 Vega/M Dark Blue/OH5SP $1.50

2010 FASTER THAN EVER 1 OF 10

❏ **Custom V-8 Vega/Pearl White/FTE..................... $3.00**
❏ Custom V-8 Vega/Pearl White/OH5SP $1.50

2010 FASTER THAN EVER 2 OF 10

❏ **Corvette Grand Sport/M Dark Red/FTE $2.00**
❏ Corvette Grand Sport/M Dark Red/OH5SP $1.50

❑ **Corvette Grand Sport/Yellow/FTE** $2.00
❑ Corvette Grand Sport/Yellow/OH5SP $1.50

❑ **Triumph TR6/M Dark Red/FTE** $2.00
❑ Triumph TR6/M Dark Red/OH5SP.................... $1.50

❑ Triumph TR6/Yellow/FTE (K-Mart) $3.00

❑ **Ford Mustang Fastback/M Silver/FTE** $3.00
❑ Ford Mustang Fastback/M Silver/OH5SP $2.00

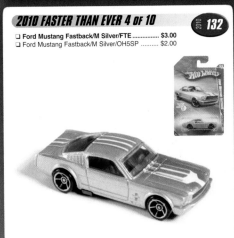

❑ Ford Mustang Fastback/Pearl Yellow/FTE (Walmart)
.... $3.00

❑ **Ford Mustang Fastback/Red/FTE** $4.00
❑ Ford Mustang Fastback/Red/OH5SP $2.00

☐ C6 Corvette/Dark Blue/FTE $4.00
☐ C6 Corvette/Dark Blue/OH5SP $2.00

☐ '67 Pontiac GTO/M Grey/FTE $2.50
☐ '67 Pontiac GTO/M Grey/OH5SP $2.00

☐ '67 Pontiac GTO/M Orange/FTE (Walmart) $3.00

☐ '67 Pontiac GTO/Pearl White/FTE $2.50
☐ '67 Pontiac GTO/Pearl White/OH5SP $2.00

☐ Fast Fish/M Silver/ $2.00
☐ Fast Fish/M Gold/FTE $2.00
☐ Fast Fish/M Gold/OH5SP $1.50
☐ Fast Fish/Red/FTE... $2.00

☐ '70 Chevy Chevelle/M Gold/FTE $3.00
☐ '70 Chevy Chevelle/M Gold/OH5SP $2.00

2010

❏ '70 Chevy Chevelle/M Green/FTE........................ $3.00
❏ '70 Chevy Chevelle/M Green/OH5SP $2.00

❏ '70 Chevy Chevelle/M Red/FTE (Walmart)..........$4.00

❏ Carbonator/Clear Orange/FTE............................ $2.00

❏ '07 Ford Shelby GT500/Dark Green/FTE $3.00
❏ '07 Ford Shelby GT500/Dark Green/OH5SP...... $2.00

❏ '07 Ford Shelby GT500/M Dark Blue/FTE............$3.00
❏ '07 Ford Shelby GT500/M Dark Blue/OH5SP $2.00

❏ '07 Ford Shelby GT500/M Red-Violet/FTE $3.00
❏ '07 Ford Shelby GT500/M Red-Violet/OH5SP.... $2.00

2010 HW HOT RODS 1 of 10 2010 139

❏ Custom '41 Willys Coupe/M Dark Red/5SP $1.50

2010 HW HOT RODS 1 of 10 2010 139

❏ Custom '41 Willys Coupe/M Green/Gold5SP (K-Mart)
.... $2.00

2010 HW HOT RODS 2 of 10 2010 140

❏ 1/4 Mile Coupe/M Green/5SP $1.50

2010 HW HOT RODS 2 of 10 2010 140

❏ 1/4 Mile Coupe/Red/5SP $1.50

2010 HW HOT RODS 3 of 10 2010 141

❏ '37 Ford Woodie/Pearl White/Orange5SP $1.50

2010 HW HOT RODS 3 of 10 2010 142

❏ '32 Ford/M Aqua Blue/5SP $1.50

❏ Bone Shaker/M Candy Red/Gold5SP $2.00

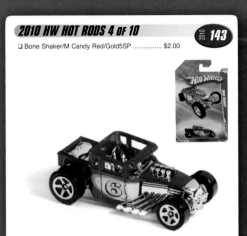

❏ Bone Shaker/Orange/5SP $2.00

❏ Bone Shaker/Satin Blue/Gold5SP $2.00
❏ Bone Shaker/Satin Blue/GY5SP (Walmart) $3.00

❏ Deuce Roadster/M Black/5SP $2.00
❏ Deuce Roadster/M Black/BFG5SP (Walmart) $3.00

❏ Straight Pipes/M Orange/5SP $2.00

❏ Straight Pipes/M Purple/5SP $2.00

2010 HW HOT RODS 8 OF 10

2010 | 146

❏ '40 Ford Pick Up/M Silver/5SP $1.50

2010 HW HOT RODS 9 OF 10

2010 | 147

❏ Sooo Fast/Dark M Blue/OH5SP $1.50

2010 HW HOT RODS 10 OF 10

2010 | 148

❏ T-Bucket/Purple/Gold5SP $1.50

2010 HW RACING 1 OF 10

2010 | 149

❏ F1 Racer/M Dark Blue/Red-BlackOH5SP $1.50

2010 HW RACING 1 OF 10

2010 | 149

❏ F1 Racer/M Dark Purple/Orange-BlackOH5SP ..$1.50

2010 HW RACING 2 OF 10

2010 | 150

❏ Circle Tracker/M Blue/Red-BlackOH5SP $1.50

2010

Beckett Price Guide to: 229

❏ Custom Ford Bronco/Pearl White/OrangeOR5SP......$1.50

❏ Custom Ford Bronco/Red/OR5SP..................... $1.50

❏ Madfast/M Blue/RedOH5SP-SK5 .... $1.50

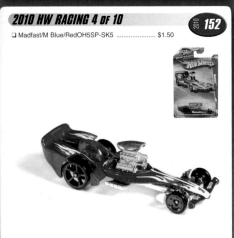

❏ Mad Propz/Black/Micro5SP $1.50

❏ **Mad Propz/M Blue/Micro5SP** **$1.50**
❏ Mad Propz/Orange/Micro5SP $1.50

❏ Ferrari F430 Challenge/M Dk Blue/WhiteY5........$2.50

2010 HW RACING 6 OF 10 154

❏ Ferrari F430 Challenge/Red/WhiteY52 .... $2.50

2010 HW RACING 6 OF 10 154

❏ Ferrari F430 Challenge/Yellow/WhiteY5 ....$3.00

2010 HW RACING 7 OF 10 155

❏ **Canyon Carver/M Dark Orange/OrangeMC3 ......$2.00**
❏ Canyon Carver/Pearl White/RedMC3 .... $2.00

2010 HW RACING 8 OF 10 156

❏ Riley & Scott MK III/M Blue/10SP $1.50

2010 HW RACING 8 OF 10 156

❏ Riley & Scott MK III/M Grey/10SP $1.50

2010 HW RACING 9 OF 10 157

❏ Ford GT LM/Green/PR5..................................... $2.00

2010

❑ **Ford Mustang Funny Car/M Purple/5SP** $1.50
❑ Ford Mustang Funny Car/M Purple/GY5SP (Walmart) $2.00

❑ Ford Mustang Funny Car/Pearl White/Gold5SP..........$1.50

❑ Ford Mustang Funny Car/Red/Gold5SP.......$2.00

❑ Custom '59 Cadillac/M Black/WSP (Walmart) $2.00

❑ Custom '59 Cadillac/M Purple/WSP $1.50

❑ Bugatti Veyron/Satin Blue/Black-ChromePR5 ....$8.00

2010

❑ Bugatti Veyron/Satin Red/10SP (Walmart) $6.00

❑ '64 Chevy Impala/M Blue/5SP $1.50

❑ **'64 Chevy Impala/M Red/5SP** $1.50
❑ '64 Chevy Impala/M Red/BFG5SP (Walmart) $2.00

❑ '55 Chevy Bel Air/M Blue/5SP $2.00

❑ '55 Chevy Bel Air/M Orange/5SP........................ $2.00

❑ **'55 Chevy Bel Air/Red/5SP** $2.00
❑ '55 Chevy Bel Air/Red/BFG5SP (Walmart) $2.50

2010

❑ '56 Merc/Lime Green-Green/5SP $1.50

❑ '56 Merc/M Lt. Purple-Purple/5SP $1.50

❑ Callaway C7/M Blue/PR5 .... $1.50

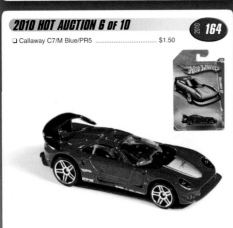

❑ Shelby Cobra 427 SC/M Dark Burgundy/10SP......... $3.00

❑ Shelby Cobra 427 SC/Pearl White/10SP $4.00

❑ **Ford Thunderbolt/M Champagne/5SP (K-Mart)......$2.00**
❑ Ford Thunderbolt/Pearl White/5SP $1.50

2010

2010 HOT AUCTION 9 OF 10 · 167

☐ Classic Nomad/M Red/5SP $2.00

2010 HOT AUCTION 10 OF 10 · 168

☐ Olds 442/M Black/PR5 (K-Mart) $5.00

2010 HOT AUCTION 10 OF 10 · 168

☐ Olds 442/Pearl Yellow/PR5 .... $4.00

2010 RACE WORLD SPEEDWAY 2 OF 4 · 170

☐ Super Modified/Pearl White/GoldWSP $1.50

2010 RACE WORLD SPEEDWAY 3 OF 4 · 171

☐ Cadillac LMP/M Gold/Red-BlackPR5 .... $1.50
☐ Cadillac LMP/M Gold/GY5SP (Walmart) $2.00

2010 RACE WORLD SPEEDWAY 4 OF 4 · 172

☐ Saleen S7/Black/Yellow-BlackOH5SP $3.00
☐ Saleen S7/Black/GY5SP (Walmart) $2.00

❏ Saleen S7/M Red/Yellow-BlackOH5SP $2.00

❏ Poison Arrow/Clear Blue/Micro5SP $1.50

❏ Tri & Stop Me/Black/MC3-OH5SP $1.50

❏ '84 Pontiac/M Dark Blue/PR5 .... $1.50

❏ '84 Pontiac/M Green/PR5 .... $1.50

❏ Flame Stopper/Orange/OR5SP............................ $1.50
❏ Flame Stopper/Orange/5SP................................ $1.50

2010

2010 RACE WORLD BEACH 1 of 4 — 177
❑ Meyers Manx/M Blue/5SP $1.50
❑ Meyers Manx/M Blue/BFG5SP (Walmart) $2.00

2010 RACE WORLD BEACH 1 of 4 — 177
❑ Meyers Manx/M Gold/5SP................................ $1.50

2010 RACE WORLD BEACH 2 of 4 — 178
❑ Deora II/M Orange/OH5SP $3.00

2010 RACE WORLD BEACH 3 of 4 — 179
❑ Sharkruiser/M Dark Grey/OH5SP $1.50

2010 RACE WORLD BEACH 4 of 4 — 180
❑ Rockster/Dark Yellow/OR5SP $1.50

2010 RACE WORLD CITY 1 of 4 — 181
❑ 5 Alarm/Flourescent Yellow/Gold-BlackPR5 ...... $2.00

2010

❏ 5 Alarm/Green/Orange-BlackPR5 .... $2.00

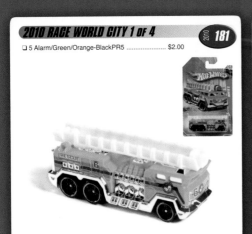

❏ Super Van/Pearl White/5SP237131 .... $2.00

❏ Propper Chopper/Green $3.00

❏ Armored Truck/Red/5SP237231 .... $2.00

❏ Fangster/M Dark Orange/5SP $2.00

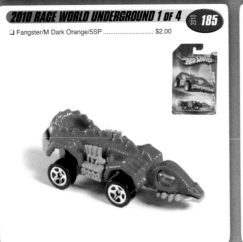

❏ Road Cannibal/M Dark Olive Green/Gold-BlackOH5SP
.... $1.50

2010

2010 RACE WORLD UNDERGROUND 4 OF 4 — 2010 | 188

❏ Enforcer/M Olive Green/5SP $1.50

2010 RACE WORLD DESERT 1 OF 4 — 2010 | 189

❏ Toyota Off Road Truck/Black/OR5SP $1.50

2010 RACE WORLD DESERT 2 OF 4 — 2010 | 190

❏ Bad Mudder 2/M Blue/OR5SP............................. $1.50
❏ Bad Mudder 2/M Blue/5SP $1.50

2010 RACE WORLD DESERT 3 OF 4 — 2010 | 191

❏ Sand Stinger/Orange/OrangeOR5SP $1.50

2010 RACE WORLD HIGHWAY 1 OF 4 — 2010 | 193

❏ OCC Splitback/M Purple/Orange-BlackMC3
....$2.00

2010 RACE WORLD HIGHWAY 1 OF 4 — 2010 | 193

❏ OCC Splitback/M Red/Gold-BlackMC3 .... $2.00

2010

❏ Bad Bagger/M Champagne/Black-ChromeMC3..........$1.50

❏ Pit Cruiser/M Silver/Orange-BlackMC3.............. $2.00

❏ Airy 8/M Black/Red-BlackMC5 .... $2.00

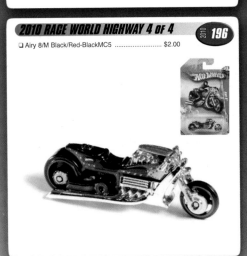

❏ Invader/M Dark Grey/Red5SP........................... $1.50

❏ Humvee/Grey/GreenOR5SP $2.00

❏ XS-IVE/Dark Blue/Orange5SP $2.00

2010

2010 RACE WORLD BATTLE 4 OF 4 2010 200

❏ **Sting Rod/Dark Olive Green/GoldOR5SP** **$1.50**
❏ Sting Rod/Dark Olive Green/GoldOH5SP $1.50

2010 RACE WORLD EARTH 1 OF 4 2010 201

❏ Nerve Hammer/Clear Red/PR5 .... $2.00

2010 RACE WORLD EARTH 2 OF 4 2010 202

❏ Scion xB/Clear Green/PR5 .... $1.50

2010 RACE WORLD EARTH 3 OF 4 2010 203

❏ Paradigm Shift/Clear Blue/OH5SP $1.50

2010 RACE WORLD EARTH 4 OF 4 2010 204

❏ Stockar/Clear/5SP $2.00

2010 RACE WORLD CAVE 1 OF 4 2010 205

❏ Rocket Box/Red/GoldPR5 .... $1.50

❏ Evil Twin/M Copper/GoldY5 .... $2.00

❏ **Phantom Racer/M Dark Violet/BFG5SP (Walmart)... $2.00**
❏ Phantom Racer/M Dark Violet/Orange-BlackOH5SP $1.50

❏ Hot Bird/M Blue/Red5SP.................................... $2.00

❏ Hot Bird/M Red/Orange5SP $2.00

❏ Twin Mill/M Black/Red-BlackPR5 .... $2.00

❏ Corvette Stingray/Satin Blue/OR5SP $3.00

2010

2010 RACE WORLD JUNGLE 2 OF 4 — 214

❏ Custom '42 Jeep CJ-2A/Khaki/GoldOR5SP-5SP $1.50

2010 RACE WORLD JUNGLE 3 OF 4 — 215

❏ **Swamp Buggy/M Dark Green/OR5SP** $1.50
❏ Swamp Buggy/M Dark Green/5SP $1.50

2010 RACE WORLD JUNGLE 4 OF 4 — 216

❏ Power Panel/M Orange/GoldOR5SP $1.50

2010 MYSTER CARS 1 OF 24 — 217

❏ Duel Fueler/M Grey/OrangeOH5SP $1.50

2010 MYSTER CARS 2 OF 24 — 218

❏ Fast FeLion/Black/5SP...$1.50

2010 MYSTER CARS 3 OF 24 — 219

❏ '70 Dodge HEMI Challenger/Yellow/Black-ChromePR5
....$3.00

2010

❏ Rigor Motor/M Green/PurpleOH5SP $1.50

❏ Nissan Skyline/M Dark Grey/OrangePR5 ....$2.00

❏ '65 Corvette/Pearl White/Black-ChromeOH5SP $2.00

❏ '70 Pontiac GTO/M Green/5SP $2.00

❏ Hyundai Spyder Concept/Black/GoldPR5 ....$1.50

❏ 16 Angels/Gold Chrome/Red-BlackPR5 ....$2.00

2010

2010 MYSTER CARS 14 of 24 — 2010 230

❏ Lotus Sport Elise/Yellow/White-BlackPR5 ....$2.00

2010 MYSTER CARS 15 of 24 — 2010 231

❏ Zotic/Satin Antifreeze/Yellow-BlackOH5SP $1.50

2010 MYSTER CARS 16 of 24 — 2010 232

❏ Jaded/Orange/5SP...$1.50

2010 MYSTER CARS 18 of 24 — 2010 234

❏ Nissan 350Z/M Purple/Green-BlackPR5 ....$2.00

2010 MYSTER CARS 20 of 24 — 2010 236

❏ HEMI Cuda/M Green/5SP $2.00

2010 MYSTER CARS 21 of 24 — 2010 237

❏ Honda Civic Si/Dark Blue/WhitePR5 ....$2.00

❏ Purple Passion/Pearl Pink/WSP $1.50

❏ Volkswagen Beetle Cup/M Silver/Blue10SP $4.00

❏ Aston Martin V8 Vantage/M Orange/Black-ChromePR5
....$5.00

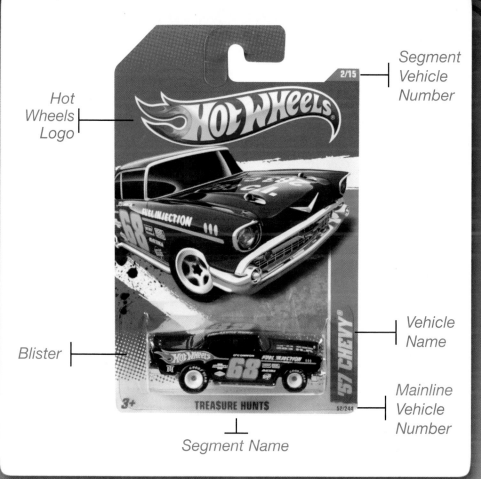

Hot Wheels Logo

Segment Vehicle Number

2/15

Blister

'57 CHEVY

Vehicle Name

Mainline Vehicle Number

S2/244

TREASURE HUNTS

Segment Name

2011 NEW MODELS 1 OF 50 — 2011 001

❏ Danicar/M Yellow/RedOH5SP $3.00

2011 NEW MODELS 2 OF 50 — 2011 002

❏ '72 Ford Gran Torino Sport/M Green/5SP $2.00

2011

2011 NEW MODELS 3 OF 50

❏ '10 Ford Shelby GT-500 Super Snake/M Blue/10SP $5.00

2011 NEW MODELS 4 OF 50

❏ '69 COPO Corvette/M Blue/OH5SP $5.00

2011 TREASURE HUNTS 2 OF 15

❏ '57 Chevy/M Midnight Blue/White5SP $30.00

2011

2011 TREA$URE HUNT$ 2 OF 15

❑ '57 Chevy/Spectraflame Midnight Blue/WhiteRR 270531 .... $50.00

2011 TRACK STARS 1 OF 15

❑ Batmobile/Flat Black/PR5 .... $3.00

2011 TRACK STARS 2 OF 15

❑ Tesla Roadster/M Lime Green/BlackPR5 .... $1.50

2011

❑ '56 Ford F-100/M Copper/Gold5SP $1.50

❑ '67 Shelby GT-500/M Red/BlackMC5 .... $4.00

❑ Chevy Pro Stock Truck/M Silver/5SP $1.50

2011 HW PERFORMANCE 1 OF 10

❑ Acura NSX/Yellow/BlackPR5 .... $1.50

2011 THRILL RACERS CAVE 6 OF 6

❑ Spider Rider/M Red/Red5SP $1.50

2011 HW VIDEO GAME HEROES 13 OF 22

❑ Shell Shock/Green/OH5SP 271331 .... $1.50

2011

COMPLETE 2011 HOT WHEELS CHECKLIST

2011 NEW MODELS

- ❏ 001 Danicar/Pearl Yellow
- ❏ 001 Danicar/Candy Red
- ❏ 002 '72 Ford Gran Torino Sport/Gang Green
- ❏ 002 '72 Ford Gran Torino Sport/Candy Red
- ❏ 003 Ford Shelby GT500 Super Snake/Blue Afflair Black
- ❏ 003 Ford Shelby GT500 Super Snake/Micro Apple Red
- ❏ 003 Ford Shelby GT500 Super Snake/Cat Yellow
- ❏ 004 '69 COPO Corvette/Dark Pearl Blue
- ❏ 004 '69 COPO Corvette/Gold Afflair White
- ❏ 004 '69 COPO Corvette/Black (Walmart)
- ❏ 005 2011 Custom Camaro/Red
- ❏ 005 2011 Custom Camaro/M Gray
- ❏ 005 2011 Custom Camaro/Mica Blue
- ❏ 006 2011 Dodge Challenger Drift Car/Micro Torch Red
- ❏ 006 2011 Dodge Challenger Drift Car/Micro Bright Blue
- ❏ 007 Fast Cash/Anodized Silver
- ❏ 008 VW Brasilia
- ❏ 009 Lamborghini Gallardo LP570-a Superleggera/Amazon Green
- ❏ 009 Lamborghini Gallardo LP570-a Superleggera/Pearl Golden Yellow
- ❏ 010 24 Ours/White
- ❏ 011 '70 Pontiac GTO Judge/Pearl Golden Yellow
- ❏ 011 '70 Pontiac GTO Judge/Lime Pearl
- ❏ 012 1971 Dodge Challenger/Sublime
- ❏ 012 1971 Dodge Challenger/Plum Crazy
- ❏ 012 1971 Dodge Challenger (Green Lantern)/Orange
- ❏ 013 Retro-Active
- ❏ 014 '63 Ford Mustang ll/Micro Medium Blue
- ❏ 014 '63 Ford Mustang ll/Pearlescent White
- ❏ 015 Speed Trap/Gold Afflair
- ❏ 015 Speed Trap/Black Black Base
- ❏ 016 Megane Trophy/Pearl Yellow
- ❏ 016 Megane Trophy/Black Black Base
- ❏ 017 Future Race DTM
- ❏ 018 Back to the Future Time Machine/Anodized Silver
- ❏ 019 Euro Racing Rig
- ❏ 020 Honda S2000/Pearl Yellow
- ❏ 020 Honda S2000/Tufflake Silver
- ❏ 021 '69 Shelby GT 500
- ❏ 022 2009 Nissan Skyline GT500
- ❏ 023 El Superfasto
- ❏ 024 Batmobile
- ❏ 025 '68 COPO Camaro
- ❏ 026 2010 BMW M3/Gold Afflair White
- ❏ 026 2010 BMW M3/Red Tint
- ❏ 027 Future Hot Rod
- ❏ 028 Buzzerk/Smoke Tint
- ❏ 028 Buzzerk/Red Tint
- ❏ 029 '63 Studebaker
- ❏ 030 Mini Challenge 1
- ❏ 031 Aston Martin One-77
- ❏ 032 Mclaren MP 4 12C
- ❏ 033 Nissan Skyline KPGC10 Race
- ❏ 034 Period Muscle
- ❏ 035 Diesel Duty
- ❏ 036 Porsche 911 GT3 RS
- ❏ 037 '10 Chevy Impala (Danica Patrick)/Process Blue
- ❏ 037 Chevy Impala (Dale Earnhardt Jr.)
- ❏ 038 Twinduction/Gold Afflair Orange
- ❏ 039 Knight Rider Pontiac Firebird
- ❏ 040 2012 Ford Fiesta
- ❏ 041 '65 Ranchero
- ❏ 042 Blown 70 Charger
- ❏ 043 2011 Dodge Charger
- ❏ 044 Alternate Vehicle 3
- ❏ 045 2011 Ferrari
- ❏ 046 Circle Trucker/Yellow Orange
- ❏ 046 Circle Trucker/Medium Turquoise
- ❏ 047 '70 Camaro Road Race
- ❏ 048 New Lamborghini
- ❏ 049 Dale Earnhardt Jr. Car
- ❏ 050 Honda HSV-010 GT

TREASURE HUNTS

- ❏ 051 Tucker Torpedo
- ❏ 051 Tucker Torpedo/Spectraflame
- ❏ 052 '57 Chevy/Micro Intense Blue
- ❏ 052 '57 Chevy/Spectraflame Blue
- ❏ 053 '58 Chevy Impala/Micro Lavender
- ❏ 053 '58 Chevy Impala/Spectraflame Pale Pink
- ❏ 054 Custom '62 Chevy Pick Up/Super Brass
- ❏ 054 Custom '62 Chevy Pick Up/M Grey
- ❏ 055 1963 Studebaker Avanti/Super Brass Gold